COUNTRIES OF THE WORLD

Iraq

Gareth Stevens Publishing
A WORLD ALMANAC EDUCATION GROUP COMPANY

About the Author: Dynise Balcavage is a freelancer writer who has visited many countries including Syria, Jordan, Israel, Morocco, and Turkey. Balcavage lives in Philadelphia with her husband, cat, and two birds.

Written by
DYNISE BALCAVAGE

Edited by
MELVIN NEO

Edited in the U.S. by
ALAN WACHTEL
LYMAN LYONS

Designed by
KENNY CHIN

Picture research by
SUSAN JANE MANUEL

First published in North America in 2003 by
Gareth Stevens Publishing
A World Almanac Education Group Company
330 West Olive Street, Suite 100
Milwaukee, Wisconsin 53212 USA

Please visit our web site at
www.garethstevens.com
For a free color catalog describing
Gareth Stevens Publishing's list of high-quality
books and multimedia programs,
call 1-800-542-2595 (USA) or 1-800-387-3178 (Canada).
Gareth Stevens Publishing's fax: (414) 332-3567.

© **TIMES MEDIA PRIVATE LIMITED 2003**
Originated and designed by
Times Editions
An imprint of Times Media Private Limited
A member of the Times Publishing Group
Times Centre, 1 New Industrial Road
Singapore 536196
http://www.timesone.com.sg/te

Library of Congress Cataloging-in-Publication Data
Balcavage, Dynise.
Iraq / by Dynise Balcavage.
p. cm. — (Countries of the world)
Summary: Provides an overview of the geography, history, government, people, arts, and foods and other aspects of life in Iraq. Includes bibliographical references and index.
ISBN 0-8368-2359-1 (lib. bdg.)
1. Iraq — Juvenile literature. [1. Iraq.] I. Title.
II. Countries of the world.
(Milwaukee, Wis.)
DS70.62.B35   2003
956.7 — dc21   2002030280

Printed in Malaysia

1 2 3 4 5 6 7 8 9 07 06 05 04 03

PICTURE CREDITS
Agence France Presse: 3 (bottom), 22, 38 (bottom), 58, 68, 74, 75, 80, 81, 82, 83 (both), 84
Art Directors & TRIP Photo Library: 5, 7, 15 (middle), 17, 18 (bottom), 29, 33, 43, 54, 55, 60, 61, 64, 65, 90 (both)
Atlas Geographic: 24
Camera Press Ltd: 59
Christine Osborne Pictures: 18 (top), 19, 79, 89
Tor Eigeland: 37, 51
Getty Images/Hulton Archive: 15 (bottom), 38 (top), 63, 69, 76, 77, 78, 83 (bottom)
Haga Library, Japan: cover, 4, 6, 32, 34, 53, 57, 72
HBL Photo Network Agency: 3 (top), 14, 16 (top), 23
Hutchison Picture Library: 20
Klingwalls Geografiska Fárgfotos: 8, 12, 13, 16 (bottom), 30, 31, 41, 44, 45, 47, 49, 50, 66, 67, 70, 73
North Wind Picture Archive: 2, 11, 56
Jaime Simson: 3 (middle), 21, 26, 48
Nik Wheeler: 1, 9, 10, 25, 27, 28, 35, 36, 39, 40, 42, 46, 52, 62, 71, 85, 87, 91

Digital Scanning by Superskill Graphics Pte Ltd

Contents

AN OVERVIEW OF IRAQ

Once part of the Ottoman Empire, the Republic of Iraq is often called the Cradle of Civilization because archaeologists have discovered in it tools dating as far back as 120,000 B.C. as well as 45,000-year-old human skeletons. Iraq's landscape features two ancient rivers, vast deserts, majestic mountains, and a view of the Persian Gulf. Just as varied are Iraq's people — Sunni Muslims, Shi'ite Muslims, Christians, Bedouins, and Kurds.

Iraq became an independent nation in 1932, and the country has been a dictatorship since 1968. Today, Iraq is most often associated with the authoritarian rule of President Saddam Hussein rather than with the country's long and colorful history and proud Islamic heritage.

Opposite: **The ancient city of Babylon served as the capital of a number of dynasties, such as the Akkadian and the Kassite.**

Below: **The Kurds are an ethnic minority who live in northern Iraq. Despite persecution by the government, life goes on as normal for most Kurds, such as this man who tends to his vegetable stall.**

THE FLAG OF IRAQ

Iraq's flag has three horizontal stripes — red, white, and black — with three green stars against the white middle stripe. The red stripe stands for courage, the white stripe represents generosity, and the black stripe stands for lands conquered by the Islamic faith. The three stars represent the countries of Iraq, Syria, and Egypt, which were once planning to unite as one. The words *Allahu Akbar* (ah-LAH-who-AHK-bar), meaning "God is great", written in the spaces between the stars, were added by President Saddam Hussein just before the start of the Persian Gulf War in 1990.

Geography

Iraq is located in the Middle East and has an area of 168,710 square miles (437,072 square kilometers). It is bordered by Turkey to the north, Iran to the east, Kuwait and the Persian Gulf to the south, Jordan and Saudi Arabia to the southwest, and Syria to the northwest. The country has 36 miles (58 kilometers) of coastline on the Persian Gulf, located on its southeastern tip.

Rivers

Two main rivers — the Tigris and the Euphrates — run through Iraq. The original name for the area between these rivers was Mesopotamia, meaning "land between two rivers." Tributaries of these rivers also flow through Iraq. The Great Zab River, for example, enters Iraq from Turkey in the north and eventually meets the Tigris near the city of Mosul.

A TALE OF TWO RIVERS

Iraq's major rivers, the Tigris and the Euphrates, provide both drinking water and water for irrigation projects. Baghdad *(below)* is one of several cities located on the Tigris River. Archaeologists have uncovered irrigation canals dug by the Sumerians who lived in the area near the Tigris around 3000 B.C.
(A Closer Look, page 72)

Mountains

The mountainous region of Iraq begins near the city of Mosul and extends to the north and east. The country's highest peak, Haji Ibrahim, rises to a height of 11,812 feet (3,600 meters). West of the mountains, the Tigris River and its tributaries have flooded the valleys to produce the rich soil that is excellent for farming.

Deserts and Plains

The southern and southwestern parts of Iraq are desert regions that spread into neighboring Syria, Jordan, and Saudi Arabia. Since the land is harsh and dry in these areas, not many people live there. Wadis, or dry stream beds, dot the desert. Whenever it rains, the wadis fill with water and become miniature rivers, which can be dangerous for the people who live in the desert.

Most of Iraq's land consists of large plains. Baghdad rests on an alluvial plain made up of sediment deposited by the Tigris and Euphrates Rivers.

Above: Iraq has a variety of landforms. In the north are rugged mountain peaks, while the southern part of the country features arid deserts. Sandwiched between these two areas are lush, green valleys.

BAGHDAD: IRAQ'S CAPITAL

Due to its strategic location, Baghdad, Iraq's largest city, has played an important role in the country's history.

(A Closer Look, page 46)

Climate

The climate in Iraq can be divided into a dry season and a wet season. Scarcely any rain falls during the dry season, which lasts from May through October. During the summer months of July and August, temperatures can reach 123° Fahrenheit (51° Celsius). The weather feels even hotter, since many areas have a high relative humidity.

Most of the country's annual rainfall occurs during the wet season between November and April. The amount of rainfall varies from region to region. The mountainous areas receive up to 40 inches (102 centimeters) of rain each year, while the southern deserts of the country receive only about 4 inches (10 cm) per year.

Iraq often experiences floods during the wet season. When rivers overflow their banks, roads become impassable and streets in some cities become too flooded and mud-covered to use. The floods also cause landslides that leave behind trails of mud and silt.

Most of Iraq does not experience harsh weather in winter. Temperatures seldom fall below freezing. In the north, however, the mountains remain snow-covered, and temperatures can dip below the freezing point.

WINDS

The *sharqi* (shar-KEE) is the ferocious wind that blows from the southern part of Iraq at speeds of more than 50 miles (80 km) per hour. When the sharqi picks up speed, a blue sky can quickly change to a reddish-brown color. The *shamal* (sham-ALL), another prevailing wind, blows between June and September, but it is not as severe as the sharqi.

Below: Temperatures in Iraq vary from region to region as a result of the terrains. These farming areas on the outskirts of the city of Mosul enjoy pleasant weather all year round, with mild summers and warm winters.

Plants and Animals

Iraq is home to a variety of vegetation. On the lower mountain slopes are hawthorns, junipers, and wild pears. In the northern part of the country, a variety of species from the sage and daisy families grow on the lower mountain slopes. The lowlands have storksbill and plantain, while willows, poplars, and licorice are found along the banks of the lower Tigris and Euphrates rivers. Throughout the country, date palms dominate the landscape, and the deserts are home to tamarisk, milfoil, and salsola.

The country is also home to a number of animal species, including the camel. Often associated with the desert, camels are known as the "ships of the desert" because they seem to float on the shifting sand dunes. This movement is possible because of their two-toed, padded feet. Camels' long eyelashes keep sand out of their eyes during sandstorms. Other animals found in Iraq are mountain goats, deer, wild pigs, wildcats, and foxes. The jerboa is a tiny, mouselike rodent that scurries across the desert sand. Also found in Iraq are hares, gazelles, and reptiles including snakes, lizards, and tortoises. Many varieties of birds live in Iraq, including vultures, hawks, and partridges.

Above: **These camels drink from a watering hole in southern Iraq. The camel is a hardy animal that can live in the desert without water for five days in summer and up to twenty-five days in winter. When food and water are scarce, the animal lives off fat that is stored in its hump.**

History

Humans have lived in northern Iraq for at least 120,000 years. Tools such as axes dating back that far have been found in the country by archaeologists.

Early Kingdoms

The people of Sumer, or the Sumerians, lived along the Tigris and Euphrates rivers between 3500 and 2400 B.C. The Sumerians, who were an advanced culture, invented the plow, the wheel, calendars, writing, and measurement systems.

The Akkadian king Sargon the Great conquered the Sumerian kingdom part by part and established the Akkadian empire in 2340 B.C. The Akkadians ruled for about two hundred years before being taken over by the Gutians, who remained in power for a century.

Between 2000 and 1800 B.C., present-day Iraq was divided between various groups that fought for control of the region. In 1792 B.C., King Hammurabi overpowered the warring factions and established a new empire called Babylonia, with its capital

SUMERIAN INVENTIONS

The origins of many tools and other important inventions used today can be traced back to the Sumerians, an ancient people that lived in the area now known as Iraq.
(A Closer Look, page 70)

Below: The Sumerians were an advanced society, and they built many temples and massive buildings. The fact that some of these structures, such as this one in Babylon, are still standing today is a testament to their understanding of building techniques.

10

Left: **This image of King Hammurabi standing before the Sun god appears on the stele on which is engraved the Code of Hammurabi. Beside stating a list of offenses, the code also stated the punishments citizens would receive if they broke the rules.**

at Babylon. Hammurabi devised a set of 282 rules called the Code of Hammurabi. Carved into a black stone called a stele, the code outlined rules concerning marriage, property, business, and slavery. The empire declined after Hammurabi's death in 1750 B.C.

The Kassites, who next took over ancient Iraq, split the country into two. The southern half of Iraq, which was called Babylon, became famous for its talented writers, whose works were read as far away as Egypt and Turkey. The northern half, called Assyria, was a leading commerce center. Many people passed through this area on their way to the Mediterranean.

The Babylonian king Nebuchadnezzar II built many exquisite structures, including the Hanging Gardens of Babylon. Waging several brutal attacks against the Egyptian pharaohs who ruled the south part of ancient Iraq, Nebuchadnezzar captured the city of Jerusalem in 597 B.C. Babylon seemed invincible; the city was surrounded by two sets of walls. In 539 B.C., however, Cyrus the Great of Persia took over the city. Later, in 320 B.C., Alexander the Great conquered what was left of Mesopotamia.

THE HANGING GARDENS OF BABYLON

Considered one of the seven wonders of the ancient world, the Hanging Gardens of Babylon derived its name from the lush landscaping within the complex.

(A Closer Look, page 56)

Arab Invasions

Modern Iraq developed when a group of Arabs known as the Abbasids conquered the area in the eighth century. Led by Abu al-Abbas as -Saffah, they made Baghdad their capital. Many students traveled to the city to study the arts, mathematics, and medicine. The age of the Abbasids came to an abrupt end in 1258, when the Mongols from central Asia invaded their country.

The Ottoman Empire

The Ottoman Turks who lived to Iraq's northwest gradually extended their control over a great deal of the region. In 1534, an Ottoman leader named Suleyman the Magnificent conquered Baghdad. With the exception of the years between 1623 and 1638, Iraq was part of the Ottoman Empire until 1917.

Modern Times

During World War I, a British force occupied Iraq. After the war, in 1920, Iraq was placed under British rule by the League of Nations. As a result of strong local resistance, the British set up a provisional government and appointed Faisal I as king.

Below: During the reign of the Abbasids, Iraq experienced a "golden age" in which the arts and culture flourished. These ruins date back to the Abbasid period.

The British gave up control of Iraq in 1932, and the country became a monarchy. The next decades were difficult ones for Iraq, as the different political groups in the country fought for contol.

Iraq joined the League of Nations in 1932. In 1945, several countries, including Iraq, formed the League of Arab States to unite Arab nations and promote cooperation among themselves.

Nuri es-Said, prime minister from 1953 to 1958, attempted to modernize Iraq but met with resistance. On July 14, 1958, members of the military staged a coup d'état. King Faisal II, Crown Prince Abd al-Ilah, and Nuri es-Said were among those killed.

The leader of this uprising, Abdul Karim Kassem, declared the country a republic and Islam the national religion. Kassem wanted the Arabs and the Kurds to work together to unify the country. Kassem's government was overthrown in 1963, and he was executed. This event marked the beginning of a succession of military coups. In 1979, Saddam Hussein became president of Iraq.

Above: **The Freedom Monument, or Nasb al-Hurriya, as it is known in Arabic, is located at Al-Tahrir Square in the heart of Baghdad. Leading Iraqi artist Jawad Salim was commissioned to design the monument, which commemorates the 1958 revolution.**

Iraq at War

In 1980, Iraq's army entered Iran and tried to claim a section of the country, causing the start of the Iran-Iraq War. Many Iraqi Kurds supported the Iranians, and at the end of the war, about sixty thousand Kurds tried to flee Iraq to safety in Iran and Turkey.

In 1990, Iraq revived a long-standing territorial dispute with Kuwait and also claimed that Kuwait was producing more oil than allowed by the Organization of Petroleum Exporting Countries (OPEC). These factors eventually led Iraq to invade Kuwait, starting the Persian Gulf War.

The Aftermath of War

After the Persian Gulf War, the United Nations declared "no-fly zones" in northern and southern Iraq to ensure the safety of the Kurdish and Shi'ite groups that lived in these areas. Economic sanctions were also imposed on Iraq to prevent Saddam Hussein from rearming his army and creating weapons of mass destruction. Relations between Iraq and the West continued to be strained as Hussein refused to comply with United Nations (U.N.) weapons inspectors and threatened to attack aircraft patrolling the no-fly zones.

THE IRAN-IRAQ WAR

The eight-year war between Iraq and Iran reflected a rivalry between the two nations for supremacy in the Persian Gulf that had deep ethnic, cultural, and territorial roots.
(A Closer Look, page 60)

THE PERSIAN GULF WAR

The invasion of Kuwait by Iraq in August 1990 caused the start of the Persian Gulf War.
(A Closer Look, page 68)

Left: **U.N. weapons inspectors in Iraq were unable to complete their missions because Saddam Hussein did not allow access to certain facilities where the inspectors suspected weapons of mass destruction were being created. The result is that economic sanctions are still in place in Iraq more than ten years after the end of the Persian Gulf War.**

Nebuchadnezzar II (c.630 B.C.–562 B.C.)

Nebuchadnezzar was king of Babylon and ruler of the New Babylonian Empire. Apart from being known for conquering the city of Jerusalem, Nebuchadnezzar was also interested in architecture. He launched many important building and renovation programs in Babylon. One of Nebuchadnezzar's most famous creations was the Ishtar Gate. Most scholars also attribute the Hanging Gardens of Babylon to the king. Although Nebuchadnezzar is remembered as a powerful king, the Book of Daniel in the Bible's Old Testament does not include a flattering description of the king. The Book of Daniel describes Nebuchadnezzar as a conceited man who suffered from mental illness.

King Faisal I

King Faisal I (1885–1933)

King of Iraq from 1921 to 1933, Faisal attended school in Constantinople (now Istanbul, Turkey). During World War I, Faisal served with the Turkish army in Syria until 1916, when he participated in an Arab revolt against the Ottomans. In 1920, a Syrian nationalist congress proclaimed Faisal king of Syria, but France, the ruling power, forced him to abdicate. In 1921, the British, who held the mandate over Iraq, nominated Faisal as king, and he was confirmed by a plebiscite. As king, Faisal helped Iraq achieve both independence and membership in the League of Nations by 1932.

Nuri es-Said

Nuri es-Said (1888–1958)

Nuri es-Said was a pro-Western leader who dominated Iraqi politics throughout the 1940s and 1950s. One of Nuri's major achievements was modernizing and preparing the country for business opportunities with other nations. Under his leadership, Iraq signed the Baghdad Pact, an alliance between Iraq and several nations, including Turkey and Pakistan, in 1955. On July 14, 1958, radical nationalists led a military coup against the government, declared Iraq a republic, and killed both Nuri es-Said and leading members of the royal family.

Government and the Economy

Iraq is divided into eighteen provinces. Three of these provinces — Arbil, As Sulaymaniyah, and Dahuk — are Kurdish and are autonomous. The country has a 250-member national assembly called the Majlis al-Watani. Thirty non-Kurds are appointed by the president to represent the three Kurdish provinces in the national assembly, while 220 members are elected by popular vote. All national-assembly members serve four-year terms.

The Ba'th Party is the only political party in the country, and it is led by Saddam Hussein. Hussein serves as both Iraq's president and prime minister. He is assisted by two vice-presidents and four deputy prime minsters.

Iraq's judicial system has three levels of courts. The country's highest court is called the Court of Cassation. Religious courts hear religious, marriage, and inheritance cases, while special courts rule on cases involving the country's security.

SADDAM HUSSEIN

Iraq's president sees himself as a visionary leader. His recent actions, however, have caused other nations to label him one of the world's most dangerous dictators.
(*A Closer Look, page 58*)

Left: As the leader of Iraq, Saddam Hussein has played a major role in shaping the nation's economy. Posters and murals depicting his image, such as this one in the city of Baghdad, can be found throughout the country.

Voting and Constitution

Iraqis above the age of eighteen may vote, but since voters must sign their names on their ballots, people do not necessarily vote for the candidates of their choice because the votes can be traced.

The elected chairman of the Revolutionary Command Council (RCC), the supreme executive, legislative, and judicial body in Iraq assumes the presidency of the country. His appointment is subject to approval by the national assembly and endorsement by a national referendum. In 1995, Saddam Hussein was approved, receiving 99.96 percent of the vote in the referendum.

Iraq's constitution, written in 1968, became effective in 1970. A new constitution drafted in 1990 was not adopted. According to the constitution, Iraqis have freedom of speech and religion and are allowed to protest and meet as they wish. The constitution also states that newspapers may print any story and that there must not be discrimination. In reality, however, Iraqis do not enjoy these freedoms.

A System of Oppression and Torture

Iraqi secret police, called the *mukhabarat* (mook-hob-BAH-rot), patrol the streets and arrest those who speak against the government. Human rights organizations have reported that the mukhabarat routinely tortures its prisoners.

IRAQ'S HIGHEST POLITICAL BODY

Eight to ten Ba'th Party officials make up the Revolutionary Command Council (RCC). A two-thirds majority vote of the RCC is needed to approve any decision, which then becomes the law. RCC members are also part of a Ba'th Party leadership body, the Regional Leadership (RL). Key political decisions are supposed to be joint decisions of the RCC and the RL. In practice, however, the decisions are made either by the president alone or by him in consultation with three to five others. The decision is then brought to a RCC meeting or a joint RCC-RL meeting for formal approval.

Economy

Much of Iraq's wealth comes from its vast oil reserves and other natural resources. The country used to earn a great deal of income from the oil industry. In 1980, Iraq was the world's second-largest oil producer, and the oil industry accounted for 95 percent of the country's income.

During the Persian Gulf War, Iraq's oil industry was severely damaged by bombs that destroyed many of its refineries and pipelines. The economic sanctions placed on Iraq by the U.N. have also affected the oil industry. In 1997, Iraq was allowed to export just enough oil to earn money to purchase medical supplies and food. In 2000, Iraq was only allowed to export oil to Switzerland, France, Russia, and China. In terms of imports, Iraq is allowed to bring in food, medicine, and some other supplies from Egypt, Russia, France, and Vietnam. The country relies on humanitarian aid from other countries for much of its food and medical supplies.

Above: Oil refineries in Iraq use tank trucks, such as this one in the city of Kirkuk, to transport oil within the country.

IRAQ'S OIL INDUSTRY

Iraq was once the world's second-largest producer of oil. The Persian Gulf War brought the country's oil industry to a standstill in the early 1990s and damaged much of the infrastructure related to the oil industry. Although pipelines and refineries such as this one in the northern Kurdish autonomous region *(left)* have been repaired, Iraq is still unable to exploit the full potential of its resources. (*A Closer Look, page 62*)

Other Natural Resources and Industries

Iraq has other natural resources including salt, natural gas, gypsum, sulfur, and phosphates. Although the country earns some money by exploiting these resources, it is not enough to improve the state of the economy.

Farming is one industry that still thrives in Iraq. Iraqi farmers grow many grains and fruits including wheat, barley, rice, grapes, melons, and dates. Before sanctions were imposed, Iraq imported much of its food, but food is now rationed.

Despite the imposition of sanctions, Iraq's banking industry continues to exist. Other than the Central Bank of Iraq, there are also nationalized commercial banks, private commercial banks, and even specialized banks. The banks assist the people with real estate transactions, business matters, and loan applications.

Other Iraqi industries include electricity, petroleum, chemicals, textiles, construction materials, and food processing.

Above: **Iraq is a producer of delicious dates that are grown on plantations such as this one located along the Shatt Al-Arab Waterway near Basra.**

ECONOMIC SANCTIONS

To prevent Iraq from buying resources to create weapons of mass destruction and rearming its military following the Persian Gulf War, the U.N. imposed economic sanctions on the country.
(A Closer Look, page 54)

People and Lifestyle

Iraq's population of over 23 million includes people from different backgrounds. Most Iraqis are Arab Muslims. Small groups of Jews and Christians also make their homes in Iraq. Most Iraqis live in large cities, as these bustling urban centers offer more employment opportunities with higher wages.

The Kurds

The Kurds, Iraq's largest ethnic minority, live in the rugged, mountainous region in the northeastern part of the country. Most Kurds are either farmers or shepherds who follow their herds of goats and sheep as they graze. Kurds stand out because they wear brightly colored attire decorated with intricate embroidery. Many Kurdish men carry *khanjars* (CAN-jars), or daggers, at their sides, although the weapons are rarely used. Kurdish women usually wear long skirts, colorful shawls, scarves, and wide belts.

THE KURDS

Despite the influence of modern technology, the Kurds of Iraq still continue practicing their traditional customs.
(*A Closer Look*, page 64)

Below: After Arabs, Kurds are the next largest ethnic group in Iraq. As shepherds and farmers, the Kurds lead a simple lifestyle, living in traditional houses. In recent times, many Kurds have moved from the rural areas to the cities in search of employment.

The Ma'dan

The *Ma'dan* (MAH-dan), or Marsh Arabs, live in the marshy area of Iraq where the Tigris River meets the Euphrates River. These people live in triangular houses made of reeds that do not have electricity, running water, or heating systems, and must be elevated to remain dry. The Ma'dan live off the land by fishing and hunting. They are known for being good hosts, and each Ma'dan village has a guest house called a *mudhif* (mood-HEEF) that is decorated with carpets and pillows.

Above: **The marshlands of southern Iraq are home to the Ma'dan, who live in houses built of reed.**

The Bedouin

The Bedouin are nomads who roam from place to place, following their herds of sheep and goats. They live in tents made of goat or camel hair. Men and women occupy separate rooms, and the women's quarters is called the harem. Similar to the Ma'dan, the Bedouin are also hospitable; they will always feed and provide shelter to a stranger, with the understanding that, one day, they might need the favor returned.

THE BEDOUIN

Nomad shepherds who make their home in the desert, the Bedouin continue to lead a lifestyle similar to that of their ancestors.
(A Closer Look, page 50)

21

Other Minority Groups

Several other minorities make their home in Iraq. The Turkomans live in the city of Mosul in southwestern Iraq and are distant relatives of the Mongols who invaded Iraq seven centuries ago. Turkomans speak a language that is similar to Turkish.

The Yazidis (yah-ZEE-deez) are a religious group who live in northwestern Iraq. Their name means "God" in Farsi, the language spoken in Iran. Yazidis study both the Bible, the holy book of Christianity, and the Qur'an, the holy book of Islam. Yazidi men often wear loose white robes and flaming red turbans.

Most Sabeans are respected boat builders who live near the rivers of southern Iraq. In fact, their religion states that they must live near a body of running water. These people are quite gentle and do not believe in war. Unlike most Middle Eastern people, Sabeans are vegetarians. A number of Sabeans live in the city of Baghdad, where they make and sell jewelry.

AT HOME

Iraqi homes are fairly private, with high walls built around houses. Each home has a formal sitting room where the family receives friends and visitors.

Below: Female members of the Yazidi community gather to meditate in the city of Mosul. The Yazidis believe they were created separately from the rest of mankind and keep themselves strictly segregated from the people among whom they live.

Family Life

Iraq has seen much instability since the 1980s, but one area that provides a great deal of stability is the family. In Iraq, families are large and usually live in the same house. When the family grows larger, an extension called a *mushtamal* (moosh-TAH-mal) is added to the main house to accommodate more family members. Most children in Iraq usually live with their parents until they are about twenty-five years old.

Funerals

Losing a loved one is a sad occasion, and Iraqis show their grief quite openly. When a person dies, his or her body is washed and then covered with a white cotton cloth. The person is then promptly buried, lying on his or her side facing Mecca, Islam's holiest city. Female relatives of the deceased stay indoors for a mourning period of forty days and wear black for an entire year.

Above: Iraqi families are close knit, and family members often spend their free time at home.

CLOTHING IN IRAQ

Although Iraqi women are not obliged to wear the *abbayah* (ah-BYE-ah), a long gown and veil, they are encouraged to dress modestly. Iraqi men also dress conservatively, wearing western-style pants and shirts. Shorts are taboo and are not allowed to be worn.

Love and Marriage

Since marriage is an important part of Iraqi life, it is rare to find single men or women. Most Iraqis do not choose their spouses, as parents usually arrange their children's weddings.

In the past, women usually got married in their early twenties, but today, more women choose to go to universities and pursue careers before they wed. This change is, in part, a result of the economic sanctions that were imposed in the early 1990s; some men cannot afford to pay a bride's dowry or raise a family. To encourage more marriages, the government pays for mass weddings in which many couples are married at the same time.

During the wedding ceremony, the bride wears a wedding gown and her hands are decorated with henna, a dye that stains the skin a reddish color. Female guests visit the bride at her father's home during the day. In the evening, guests participate in traditional dances. The groom signs the marriage contract at the home of the bride's father.

Although Muslim men may have as many as four wives, most men these days only have one wife. This is partly because having many wives is expensive and partly because the practice of having four wives is considered old-fashioned.

**BASRA:
AN ECONOMIC AND
CULTURAL CENTER**

Located on the Shatt al-Arab Waterway, Basra, Iraq's second-largest city, is an important cultural and economic hub.
(A Closer Look, page 48)

Below: In a traditional Iraqi wedding, such as this one in the city of Basra, the bride *(center)* is completely covered as she steps out of her father's home.

Above: **Iraqi children often attend extra classes, such as this art class held in a public library in Baghdad.**

Education

In 1850, only 1 percent of Iraqis were literate. Today, more than 58 percent of the population can read and write, as schooling is compulsory between the ages of six and eleven. About half of all Iraqi students go on to high school. Education is considered important, and even tiny villages have schools. Children attend school for free, and provided they meet the standards, can even continue to study up to the college level. Both men and women teach in the Iraqi school system. Unlike some Arab countries, Iraq openly encourages women to pursue education.

Iraq has eight universities. Four are in Baghdad, while the others are in Al Basra, Arbil, Mosul, and Tikrit. The country also has twenty-two institutions that specialize in teaching farming, technology, and administration.

MOSUL: CITY OF DIVERSITY

Mosul is made up of people of various cultures. Its architecture is just as varied, ranging from ruins to modern residential complexes.

(A Closer Look, page 66)

Religion

Islam is the official religion of Iraq, and 97 percent of the population is Muslim. Between 60 to 65 percent of the nation's Muslims are Shi'ite, while 32 to 37 percent are Sunni Muslims. Three percent of the population is non-Muslim. These people are allowed to practice their own religions within certain guidelines.

The Five Pillars of Islam

Islam has five main rules, called the Pillars of Islam. The first pillar is *shahada* (SHA-hah-dah), or the declaration of faith. All Muslims must declare "There is no god but Allah, and Muhammad the prophet is his messenger." The second pillar is *salah* (SALL-ah), or prayer. Muslims are required to pray five times a day facing Mecca, Islam's holiest city. In Iraq, businesses must close during prayer times, which are printed in the newspapers. The third rule is *zakat* (zah-COT), or giving alms to the poor. Next is *sawm* (SAH-m), or fasting. During the month of Ramadan, Muslims do not eat, drink, or smoke between sunrise and sunset. The final pillar requires that Muslims make a hajj, or pilgrimage to Mecca, at least once in their lifetime.

CHRISTIANS IN IRAQ

Although most Iraqis are Muslims, Christians have lived and worshiped in this desert country for about 2,000 years.
(A Closer Look, page 52)

Below: Islam has been practiced in Iraq since the seventh century. As a result, the country has a number of historic mosques. With its gold colored dome and minarets, the Mosque of Iman Ali, in the city of An Najaf, is a fine example of Islamic architecture.

Shi'ite and Sunni Muslims

Most Iraqis are Shi'ite Muslims, but the rulers of the country are Sunni Muslims. The difference between these two groups lies in whom they accept as the leaders of Islam. Shi'ites believe that Islamic leaders must be relatives of the prophet Muhammad and that the current leader must name the next leader. Sunnis believe anyone qualified may serve as the religious leader.

Superstitions

Iraqis can be superstitious, and some follow certain rituals to protect themselves from bad luck. For example, a family experiencing a period of bad luck may feel they have been struck by the evil eye. In order to make the evil eye go away, household members wear amulets with evil eye symbols. Symbols of the evil eye, often blue glass decorations, are often hung in homes and cars.

To bring good luck, many Iraqis display an oak apple in a gold frame in much the same way people in the West might carry a rabbit's foot or other lucky charm.

Above: **Iraq is a Muslim nation, but people of other faiths are allowed, within certain restrictions, to practice their own religions. On Sundays, Christians attend services in churches such as the Church of Tahira in the city of Qaraqosh.**

Language and Literature

With its curving letters that feature loops, dots, and twirls, Arabic script is a joy to view. Arabic, read from right to left, is Iraq's official language. It is also spoken throughout the Middle East and in North Africa.

The Arabic alphabet has twenty-eight different letters. Accent marks in words tell speakers how to pronounce the words. Arabic letters are written differently depending on whether they are at the beginning, middle, or end of a word. Arabic numbers are also written using this script.

Spoken Arabic is difficult to imitate because it contains many guttural sounds, or sounds that come from the throat, and can appear quite harsh to a non-native speaker.

Left: **As most Iraqis are able to read, book stalls such as this one in front of the Kadhimain Mosque in Baghdad are a common sight.**

Literature

Because some of the earliest examples of writing — dating from 3000 B.C. — were found in the ancient city of Uruk, scholars believe that written language originated in the land that is now Iraq.

Many great Middle Eastern authors and poets have come from Iraq. A talented writer in the mid-700s was Rabi'a al-Adawiyya, a woman from Basra. Scholars believe that Rabi'a was a free person sold into slavery when her parents died. Rabi'a was later freed, and to give thanks to Allah, she taught and wrote about Islam until her death in A.D. 801. Today, other female poets follow in her footsteps. Nazik al-Mala'ika (1922–) is considered a radical in the Arabic poetry world, as she writes in free verse.

Muhammad Mahdi al-Jawahiri (1900–1997), one of Iraq's most famous poets, wrote about political ideas. When Muhammad attended a poetry festival in Saudi Arabia, Saddam Hussein took away his right to return to Iraq. Muhammad moved to Syria where he lived until his death at the age of ninety-seven.

Above: **Antique copies of the Qur'an are included in the collections of most museums in Iraq. This example of the Islamic holy book is written in beautiful Arabic calligraphy.**

THE DAILY NEWS

Iraq's many privately run newspapers were closed by the government in 1967. Today, there are four government-run dailies, of which the *Ath-Thawra*, the newspaper of the Ba'th Party, has the largest circulation.

Arts

In the past, Iraqis excelled as architects, potters, painters, musicians, and weavers. This rich tradition still exists today.

Iraq's art is largely dictated by Islam. Islam does not allow artists to portray images of people in their work. This means that work such as portraits are not allowed.

Most Iraqi art today still features the traditional geometric and floral shapes and designs called arabesque. Modern works, such as the Monument to the Revolution in Baghdad, are simple in design but still attractive, and they convey a powerful image.

Museums

Baghdad has several museums that house sculptures, paintings, and artifacts. Iraq nurtures its artists, and the National Museum of Modern Art in Baghdad regularly commissions local artists to produce works of art. Artists often exhibit their works in public, provided the subject matter portrayed is deemed appropriate by government censors

Below: Iraq has a strong artistic tradition, and the citizens have an appreciation for painting, sculpture, and music. This artist paints contemporary landscapes in his shop in the city of Baghdad.

Above: **Throughout Baghdad, modern skyscrapers coexist in harmony with designs from centuries past.**

Architecture

Iraq has many beautiful buildings and monuments. These include new structures with modern designs as well as grand old buildings in traditional styles. Concerned that contemporary Iraqi architecture was becoming too westernized, Saddam Hussein recently dictated that architects should try to follow pure Iraqi designs.

Beautiful Handwriting

Arabic calligraphy — with its patterns of curves, dots, and swirls — is beautiful to look at. As a result, it is a popular art form in Iraq. Many Iraqis decorate their homes with tiles, plaques, and plates that are adorned with quotes from the Qur'an. Calligraphy is also featured on sculptures, fabrics, and paintings, as well as in mosques and other buildings throughout the country.

Calligraphers often color the spaces between the letters gold, red, or blue. Sometimes the letters are even written in a manner so as to form shapes such as triangles or circles.

Music and Dance

Traditional Iraqi music features a great deal of chanting, hand-clapping, and drumming. The *oud* (OUD), which is shaped like a gourd, is one popular musical instrument. The *rebaba* (rah-BAH-bah) is a one-stringed, fiddle-like instrument played by the Bedouin. Usually, a tambourine called a *rigg* (RIG-g) keeps the beat and adds accents.

Iraqis enjoy listening to music on Radio Baghdad. The country's most popular singer is Kazem Al-Saher, who released his twelfth album, *The Impossible Love*, in 2001.

Folk dancing is a popular form of entertainment in Iraq and each region has its own dances. During the Kurdish New Year and at wedding celebrations, the Kurds take part in a circular dance. The single women dance wearing brightly colored clothes to attract their future husbands. Single men perform the same circular dance, but the men dance faster than the women and yell out in trills.

Below: **Folk dancing is popular among Iraqis, and it is regarded as both entertainment and a form of exercise.**

Hagallah is a folk dance performed by the Bedouin during the date harvest, which is also the "wedding season." In the Iraqi version, the dance starts when the men form a line and begin to clap and sing together. A veiled woman dances to the front of the line and shimmies up and down the line in tiny steps, holding a sword. The men try to remove the dancer's veil, and she stops them using her sword.

Above: **Traditional Iraqi musical instruments include the oud, the rebaba, and the rigg, as well as various hand drums.**

Venues for Artists and Arts Lovers

Young musicians and dancers perfect their skills at Baghdad's Music and Ballet School. Music and theater lovers can attend concerts performed by the National Symphony Orchestra or watch plays at the National Theater.

Many festivals held throughout Iraq also feature theatrical performances. At the Regional Festival for the Theater of Iraqi Children, guests enjoy performances by students of the Iraqi Music and Ballet School, who perform a series of ten plays.

A recent work to hit the Iraqi stage is based on a novel written by Saddam Hussein. Performed at the National Theater, the musical *Zabibah and the King* is based on Hussein's story of an unhappy, married girl who falls in love with her king.

Leisure and Festivals

Iraqis work very hard. The work week in Iraq is from Saturday through Thursday, and most people take only one day off. After work and on Fridays, they are happy to indulge in a little well-deserved relaxation.

Just like in most other Middle Eastern countries, Iraqi social life is centered around the family and close friends. Before the Persian Gulf War, Iraqis spent their days off visiting family or going to a museum or concert together. Their favorite pastimes are watching movies and television, reading, and listening to music. Backgammon and chess are popular games in Iraq, and most households have sets for playing these games.

Unfortunately, the aftermath of war and the imposition of economic sanctions has greatly affected daily life in Iraq. Now, people tend to leave home only when necessary. There is also little money for leisure activities. Many Iraqis have lost family members and friends who fought as part of the military.

Below: **A group of friends meet up in Baghdad on their day off. As Islamic society is conservative, it is unusual to see single men and women socializing in public.**

Big festive celebrations, which were commmon in the past, are practically non existent now.

Iraqi men usually work from 8:30 A.M. to 1:00 P.M., and from 4:00 P.M. to 7:00 P.M. Today, there is little information about how Iraqis spend their leisure time, as foreigners are not allowed to enter the country. In the past, before the Persian Gulf War, Iraqi men often stopped in cafés during their lunch breaks or after work, to discuss current events with friends or read newspapers while enjoying a cup of sweet tea or coffee.

Iraqi women would visit friends and relatives. Since Iraqi women spend a great deal of time at home, their hobbies often include decorating and cooking.

During their free time, Iraqi children participate in sports or dance, attend music classes, and play chess and backgammon.

In Iraq, a handshake is used both when you greet friends and when you say goodbye to them. Women may also kiss their close female friends on both cheeks.

Above: **With a three-hour-long lunch break, Iraqi men often have time to play a game of backgammon.**

Sports

Soccer is Iraq's most popular sport, and almost every neighborhood has its own amateur team. Soccer games take place in school yards and parks across the country. Soccer fans also fill the main stadium in Baghdad to watch professional matches. Cafés and restaurants have televisions that broadcast matches played between the national league teams, and spirited fans cheer their teams on to victory.

Iraqis also love team sports such as basketball and volleyball, as well as individual sports including weightlifting and boxing. Televised broadcasts of these sporting events attract large audiences. In addition, women in Iraq compete in such sports as gymnastics, volleyball, badminton, and swimming, and they regularly compete in international competitions such as the Muslim Women's Games. These games were established to give female athletes from strict Islamic countries the opportunity to take part in international competition.

Below: **Because Iraqis enjoy playing and watching a variety of sports, the government often organizes competitive events. This colorful mass display in Baghdad's national stadium marks the start of the annual Police Games.**

Left: The falcon has extraordinary hunting talents and is used by the Bedouin to hunt for game in the desert. The bird's sharp, hooked claws, stout necks, and sharp bill help it attack and kill its prey.

Falconry

Some Iraqis participate in the sport of falconry, in which they train falcons to hunt small animals such as rabbits and jerboas. As the falcon perches on the owner's forearm, the owner wears a thick glove to protect his hand and arm from the bird's sharp claws. The bird's head is covered by a tiny hood to keep it calm until hunting time. After the falcon catches its prey, the bird stands near it to guide the owner to the prey. The owner then gives the falcon a special treat as a reward for completing its task. Usually, the birds and owners develop close relationships.

Holidays

Iraq has several official secular holidays during which all public offices, businesses, and schools are closed. The holidays are New Year's Day (January 1), Army Day (January 6), Revolution Anniversary Day (February 8), FAO Day (April 17), Labor Day (May 1), National Day (July 14), Ba'th Revolution Day (July 17), and Peace Day (August 8).

Religious Festivals

Iraqis also observe all major Muslim holidays. These holidays fall on different days each year, depending on the Islamic calendar.

The holy month of Ramadan takes place in the ninth month of the Muslim calendar. During this period, healthy adult Muslims fast between sunrise and sunset. At the end of Ramadan, Muslims celebrate *Eid al-Fitr* (EAD al-FIT-er), a three-day-long festival that celebrates the breaking of the fast. After a month of abstinence, Iraqis indulge in large amounts of food.

Eid al-Adha (EAD al-AD-hah) is a festival that celebrates devout Muslims' holy pilgrimage to Mecca in Saudi Arabia. During this

Above: **Muslim women say their prayers as they celebrate the Eid al-Fitr festival that marks the end of the month of Ramadan.**

Below: **Members of the Ba'th Party take part in a parade in Baghdad to celebrate the 39th Revolution Anniversary Day on February 8, 2002.**

festival, families often slaughter a goat or sheep and donate its meat to the poor in order to show their devotion to Allah. A feast is also held for family members returning from the hajj.

Iraqis celebrate the prophet Muhammad's birthday. Iraq's Shi'ite population also celebrates *Ashura* (ah-SHOO-rah). This unusual Shi'ite holiday remembers a religious martyr named Imam Hussein, who was put to death for his religious beliefs. On Ashura, devout Shi'ites beat themselves with chains, and even barbed wire, in remembrance of Imam Hussein.

Above: **While some Iraqi festivals have an international appeal and attract participants from around the world, local festivities are also organized. These girls are marching in a street parade held in the city of Mosul to mark the arrival of spring.**

Other Festivals

Several important festivals are organized in Iraq. Each year artists and writers from all over the globe participate in the Babylon Art Festival, held in the city of Babel. Baghdad's Marbid Festival is attended by more than two hundred poets, intellectuals, and academics from ten Middle Eastern countries. During the Al-Khatma Festival, a religious celebration, the entire Qur'an is recited word-for-word.

Food

Iraqi cuisine is delicious, featuring an interesting blend of influences. Iraqis enjoy eating vegetables stuffed with rice, meats, or bulgur, and they are not afraid of mixing fruit and meat in one dish. Like most people in the Middle East, Iraqis adore rice, yogurt, and pita bread. Their dishes do not contain pork or alcohol, as these two items are forbidden by Islam. In recent times, however, the economic sanctions imposed on Iraq have created severe food shortages, forcing people to make do with what they can get.

Favorite Foods

Kabobs, or skewered chunks of grilled lamb, beef, chicken, or fish, are an Iraqi staple. One Iraqi specialty, called *masgouf* (MAS-goof), is made with fish from the Tigris River. *Quzi* (KOO-zee), or stuffed roasted lamb, and *kibba* (kih-BAH), or fried balls of ground meat, nuts, raisins and spices, are also popular. All meals include the traditional Iraqi bread called *samoons* (SAH-moons).

Left: **Masgouf is a traditional fish dish in Iraq. A cleaned, gutted fish is slowly grilled over a fire made from sweet woods before being served on a plate of sliced onions and tomatoes, together with slices of bread.**

After dinner, some Iraqis enjoy Arabic coffee served in a small glass, while others prefer strong, sweet tea. Iraqis have a sweet tooth and like rich desserts such as *baklava* (baa-KLAH-vah), a rich pastry made of layers of honey, thin sheets of buttery dough, and nuts. Dates in syrup, or *murabba amar* (moor-ah-bah AH-mar), date pastries, or *zlabiya* (zlah-BEE-yah), and fresh fruits are also popular dessert choices.

Above: **In the 1980s, Iraq used to import much of its food, and lavish spreads such as this were common. The country's economy, however, collapsed after the Persian Gulf War, and today Iraqis barely have enough money to buy basic food staples such as rice and cooking oil.**

Iraqi Hospitality

An Iraqi hostess feeds her guests large servings, but she does not eat with her guests. Instead, the hostess tends to guests' needs, making sure there is enough to eat and drink. Dessert and coffee are usually served in a different room than the main meal. When it is time for the guests to leave, the hostess sprinkles some rose water on top of each guest's head. This is done so that guests will take away the sweet memory of the meal and think of her whenever they smell the scent of roses.

A CLOSER LOOK AT IRAQ

After gaining its independence in 1932, Iraq was declared a republic in 1958. The country boasts a rich and colorful history. The ancient civilizations that occupied what is present-day Iraq have left their mark on the land. Building ruins and archaeological sites throughout the country provide insight into the life and culture of generations past. Architectural construction from the twelfth century onward also provides archaeologists with significant clues about the region's rich heritage.

Iraq's importance, however, is not just in its ancient history. The nation has also played a key role in recent world events. Since coming under the leadership of Saddam Hussein in 1979, the country has been in two wars. Iraq initiated both the eight-year-long Iran-Iraq War and the Persian Gulf War. Today, the aftermath of the Persian Gulf War is still felt by the Iraqis as a result of economic sanctions imposed by the U.N., and Saddam Hussein remains among the world's most feared dictators.

Opposite: In Iraq, great emphasis is placed on education. These Ma'dan women attend a special school for mothers.

Below: The beautiful landscape of northern Iraq is dotted with ruins of houses. Once the homes of Iraqi Kurds, these ruins stand as a silent reminder of the people who have been tortured, persecuted, and even murdered by Saddam Hussein's government.

Archaeological Sites

Iraq is considered the cradle of civilization because many of the country's archaeological treasures shed light on the world's first societies. Home to some ten thousand archaeological sites, even more sites are believed to be lying undiscovered beneath its surface. As recently as June 2001, archaeologists uncovered an Assyrian temple and sculptures in northern Iraq that date back to 900 B.C.

The Arch of Ctesiphon

Believed to have been built during the reign of Sasanian king Khosrow I, who ruled from A.D. 531 to 578, the Arch of Ctesiphon formed part of the front of the royal palace. The arch is approximately 115 feet (35 m) high and 82 feet (25 m) wide, and it is the only surviving remnant of the ancient Parthian city that was located southeast of modern-day Baghdad.

The Palaces of Nimrud

Perhaps the country's most famous archaeological site is Nimrud, which was formerly the ancient Assyrian capital known as Calah.

Below: **This carving of a mythical winged beast is situated at the entrance of the Palace of Ashurnasirpal II (c. 800 B.C.) at Nimrud.**

Starting in 1845, British archaeologist Sir Austen Henry Layard, who was followed by Sir Max Mallowen, unearthed Assyrian palaces dating back to between 900 and 700 B.C. The gates of one of these palaces feature sculptures of hawk-winged lions with human heads. These palaces offered the kings comfort from the hot desert sun through an early form of air-conditioning.

Ur

Dating back to 4000 B.C., Ur was an important city of ancient southern Mesopotamia and is widely believed to have been the birthplace of Abraham. Once the capital of ancient empires, the city was abandoned between 300 and 200 B.C. Lying undiscovered for thousands of years, parts of the city were unearthed by British archaeologist J.E. Taylor in the 1880s. More extensive excavations were carried out after World War 1 by H.R. Hall and then from 1922 to 1934 by Leonard Woolley. Discoveries from the site have provided us with a wealth of information about Mesopotamian history and culture.

One of the most fascinating discoveries at Ur is the royal cemetery. The tombs of the ancient kings and queens were filled with gold, silver, and bronze items and were decorated with precious gems. In addition, attendants were also buried in the tombs so they could serve their master or mistress in the afterlife.

LOST THROUGH WAR

As a result of the wars that have plagued Iraq in recent years, many of the country's priceless archaeological treasures have been damaged or destroyed. In addition, foreign scientists and archaeologists are no longer allowed to visit the country's archaeological sites. Many artifacts that are uncovered are often smuggled out of the sites and sold on the black market by Iraqis desperate to earn money.

Baghdad: Iraq's Capital

Located on the fertile banks of the Tigris River, Baghdad — Iraq's capital and largest city — is home to more than four million people. Founded in A.D. 762 by Caliph al-Mansur, Baghdad quickly developed into an important city due to its strategic location at the crossroads of many ancient trade routes.

Today, Baghdad combines contemporary buildings with historic wonders. The thirteenth-century Al-Mustansiriya Madrasah Mosque and the tenth-century minaret of Suq al-Ghazi stand harmoniously near the modern buildings of the University of Baghdad. Until economic sanctions were imposed in the early 1990s, Baghdad was a busy trade city and an important Middle Eastern economic center.

A Colorful History

Baghdad was at its peak during the reigns of al-Mahdi and Harun ar-Rashid in the eighth and ninth centuries. After Harun ar-Rashid's

Below: **In the older parts of Baghdad, the narrow streets are flanked by traditional houses, such as these in the Qadiman district.**

death, the city's importance gradually declined. The Mongols pillaged Baghdad in 1258, Timur raided the city in 1401, and the Persian shah Isma'il I raided it in 1508. Baghdad was also weakened by constant Persian and Turkish invasions until 1534, when it finally became part of the Ottoman Empire. In 1917, during World War I, the British took over Baghdad. The city became the capital of Iraq in 1921, when Faisal I became king.

A Cultural Paradise

Baghdad is home to many cultural treasures. These wonders include the magnificent Abbasid Palace overlooking the Tigris River; the Iraqi Museum, which is the largest museum in the Middle East; and the Al-Khadhimain Mosque, which is famous for its gold-capped domes and minarets.

Baghdad was once called the City of Peace, but extensive bombing during the Persian Gulf War has destroyed much of the city. Although many monuments and buildings were reconstructed, these replacements do not project the splendor of the originals.

Above: **Iraq has a rich cultural history, and the country's many museums, such as Baghdad Museum, were filled with artifacts dating back to prehistoric times. Today, however, the condition of its museums is uncertain, as the Iraqi government forbids foreigners from entering the country.**

Basra: A Cultural and Economic Center

Located in southeastern Iraq, Basra is the country's second-largest city and the capital of Al Basrah province. The city is located on the Shatt Al-Arab Waterway, about 71 miles (114 km) from the Persian Gulf. Before the imposition of economic sanctions, oil shipping and refining and the manufacture of petrochemicals and fertilizers were the foundation of the city's economy.

The city was founded by Caliph Umar I in A.D. 638 as a military base. Basra flourished under the rule of the Abbasids but in later centuries, fell into a state of decline. Many battles between the Turks and invading Persians and Marsh Arabs took place here.

During the sixteenth century, Basra enjoyed a rebirth when it became an important port for Arab trading ships on their way to the Far East. In 1624, Caliph Ali Pasha fought off a Persian attack, and Basra enjoyed a short period of peace and stability.

Below: **Traditional houses, some of which have wooden balconies overlooking streets, are found throughout the city of Basra.**

Basra was occupied by the British during World Wars I and II, and the city served as an important point along the Allied supply route to the former Soviet Union. After World War II, Basra flourished due to its port and nearby oil fields.

Above: **By virtue of Basra's location along the Shatt Al-Arab Waterway, the city has played an important role in Iraq's trade with other countries.**

A City of Neighborhoods

The unique qualities of Basra are reflected in its three major neighborhoods. Ashar, an ancient business district, houses many mazelike bazaars and a beachside site called the Corniche. Many historic homes in this area feature wooden balconies that hang over the streets. Margil is a port located in Basra, and many Iraqis live in contemporary houses and apartments located in this district. In the area called Basra Proper, traditional houses still line the streets of an ancient neighborhood.

Basra Today

Basra remains an important Iraqi cultural center. People from all over the country visit its museums. The Floating Navy Museum is filled with items collected during the Iran-Iraq War, while history enthusiasts enjoy the Basra Museum with its Sumerian, Babylonian, and Islamic collections.

The Bedouin

The word *Bedouin* means "one who lives in the desert" in Arabic and, indeed, the Arabic-speaking Bedouin are desert nomads. The Bedouin are also found throughout the Middle East and in North Africa. Most Bedouin are either farmers or shepherds who keep flocks of goats, camels, and sheep. One unusual group is the Marsh Bedouin of southern Iraq, who make their home in the swamps and raise water buffaloes. Many Bedouin, including those found in Iraq, still follow a traditional lifestyle, living in tents constructed using fabrics woven from animal hair.

Families on the Move

Although some Bedouin now traverse the desert dunes using four-wheel-drive vehicles, many still use camels to navigate the sands. Typically, a Bedouin family stays in one place until its flocks have eaten most of the area's grasses — a period of around

Below: **Today, many Bedouin still follow their traditional lifestyle and tend to flocks of goats and camels. This group of Bedouin allows its animals to graze at an area near Lake Hawr al Hammar.**

Above: Bedouin children lead simple lives, as they usually follow their parents' nomadic way of living.

two months — before moving to the next location. In just one year, Bedouin families may travel up to 620 miles (998 km).

Bedouin eat mainly dairy products, which they get from their animals. Milk is an important staple. Salt is sprinkled on leftover milk so that it will not spoil. A type of cheese is also made from goats' milk.

In spring, Bedouin families enjoy a special treat — truffles, a fungus considered a delicacy all over the world. Other popular foods include bulbs, roots, rice, tomatoes, peppers, and eggs. Depending on their location, Bedouin might also grind up dried locusts to make a type of flour or simply eat the insects fried.

Rooted in Tradition

All Bedouin dress modestly in clothes that cover their bodies and heads. Bedouin men wear long cloths held in place with ropelike black bands. They also carry daggers that are rarely used. Bedouin women wear veils, decorate their faces with blue tattoos, and adorn the palms of their hands with designs made in henna. At night families sing songs accompanied by a rebaba. They also tell stories and recite poems to pass the time.

Christians in Iraq

According to tradition, the Garden of Eden that is mentioned in the book of Genesis in the Old Testament of the Bible was located in Iraq. Although Islam is the country's official religion, Christians have lived and worshiped in this desert country for about two thousand years and maintain a strong sense of history and tradition.

A Suppressed Minority

Roman Catholics make up the majority of the 700,000 Christians in Iraq. Other Christian denominations represented in the country include Assyrian Orthodox, Assyrian Catholic, Greek Orthodox, and Protestant.

In Iraq, Christians are allowed to practice their religion but are not allowed to spread their faith or conduct services outside of churches. Prayer meetings or Bible study groups at home are also forbidden by the government.

Most Iraqi Christians live in Baghdad and Mosul, as these large cities offer more job opportunities. Since the Gulf War, many of them have emigrated to the United States and Canada.

Below: **Christians in Iraq are permitted to follow the customs of their religion. Here, a priest conducts a baptism ceremony at Tahira Church in the city of Qaraqosh.**

Some Iraqi Christians are able to speak Aramaic, the ancient language that Jesus Christ spoke. The use of Aramaic, however, is gradually dwindling among younger Iraqi Christians.

Above: **The small number of churches in the city of Baghdad serves a dedicated population who follow the teachings of various Christian denominations.**

A Special Tradition

Iraqi Christians believe that the disciple John kept a piece of bread from the communion loaf that Christ shared with his apostles the night before he was crucified. Before the next communion, John added the original piece of bread into the batter for the second loaf. In turn, each baker saved a piece of dough from the original loaf to include in the next loaf. This tradition continues today.

The Pope's Visit

Pope John Paul II, the head of the Roman Catholic Church, visited Iraq in 2000. Besides praying for the country's Christians, the Pope also visited sites related to the patriarch Abraham, a figure who features prominently in both Christianity and Islam.

Economic sanctions

In 1990, when the Persian Gulf War began following Iraq's invasion of Kuwait, the U.N. and the international community imposed economic sanctions on Iraq. These sanctions prohibited nearly all trade with Iraq.

The sanctions were designed to prevent Saddam Hussein's government from buying resources to rearm its military and create weapons of mass destruction. These sanctions have curtailed Hussein's power, but have also seriously affected the Iraqi population, as food is now rationed and medicine is difficult to obtain. Later, a U.N. program allowed Iraq to purchase limited amounts of food and medicine for its citizens.

Another problem is that sanctions have caused prices to rise. Today, the standard of living for most Iraqis is about half what it was before the Persian Gulf War.

Below: **Since food is scarce in Iraq, the government has set up a food rationing system to ensure fair distribution.**

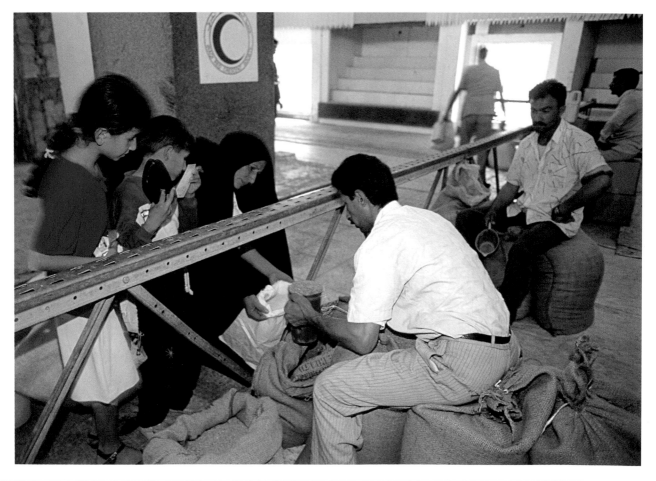

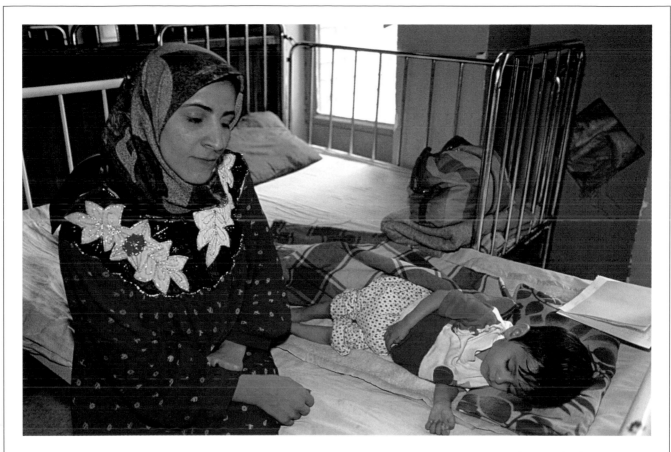

Above: **The hospitals in Iraq that still manage to operate lack sufficient funds to purchase desperately needed medical supplies.**

Although Hussein states that his people are malnourished, Iraq exports some food illegally. In April 1999, a U.N. ship discovered another ship, the M/V *Minimare*, transporting 2,600 tons (2,360 metric tonnes) of rice that Iraq was selling illegally.

Since Iraq has scarce monetary funds, the country's water and sanitation services are in desperate need of repair. As water is easily contaminated, many people, especially babies and the elderly, get sick from bacteria and viruses.

The environment in Iraq has also been seriously affected. Raw sewage is dumped into rivers, and mounds of garbage pile up in the streets because there are insufficient working garbage trucks to collect the garbage.

Are the Sanctions Working?

Saddam Hussein remains in power, lives in luxury, and has managed to continue to fund his military, while the Iraqi people suffer under the sanctions. As of August 2002, Hussein still refuses to cooperate with U.N. arms inspectors who want to search certain areas within Iraq for weapons of mass destruction.

The Hanging Gardens of Babylon

The Seven Wonders of the Ancient World include some of humankind's most amazing artistic creations. One of these ancient wonders was the Hanging Gardens of Babylon, located 31 miles (50 km) south of present-day Baghdad.

According to a Greek legend, the Assyrian queen Semiramis, who ruled from 810 to 805 B.C., commissioned the building of the Hanging Gardens of Babylon. Another legend says that Nebuchadnezzar II built the gardens as a gift to his wife, Amytis.

Left: **This print, made using an ancient hand-colored woodcut, depicts the Hanging Gardens of Babylon.**

Archaeologists believe the gardens were built on a series of terraces that climbed the sides of the royal palace. The view from the garden's 23-foot-high (7 m) wall was majestic and provided a view of the city's Tower of Babel.

According to archaeologists the gardens measured 400 feet (122 m) wide by 400 feet (122 m) long and stood more than 80 feet (24 m) high. Filled with palm trees and flowers, the gardens were named for the many trailing plants that hung from their walls and terraces. The plants thrived in the dry environment as a result of a brilliant system of irrigation. A series of water engines and chain pumps that were operated by hand pulled water from the Euphrates River into the garden. The water collected in a pool at the top of the garden and then trickled down to water the plants.

Architects have questioned why the building foundation did not crumble because of the continuous moisture. Historians have guessed that a drain was created on each terrace that directed the flow of the water away from the fragile bricks.

Above: **The ruins of the Hanging Gardens of Babylon provide an idea of the scale of the magnificent structures that supported the numerous plants in the garden.**

Saddam Hussein

Saddam Hussein was born in Tikrit in 1937. Hussein's parents were Sunni Muslims who claimed to be descendents of the Muslim prophet Muhammad.

Hussein moved to Baghdad in 1955. He became involved in politics and joined the Ba'th Party, taking part in many of its revolutionary activities. After a failed Ba'th assasination attempt on president Abdul Karim Kassem, Hussein fled the country to Egypt. He returned to Iraq in 1963. After a successful coup attempt by the Ba'th Party in 1968, Hussein became chief aide to President Ahmad Hassan al-Bakr and deputy chairman of the Revolutionary Command Council (RCC). When President al-Bakr resigned in 1979, Hussein became the new president of Iraq and, subsequently, chairman of the RCC.

At the start of his rule, Hussein saw himself as a visionary leader, and his initial goal was to modernize Iraq. As a result,

Left: **Saddam Hussein has been president of Iraq since 1979. He makes frequent public appearances and his image is captured on murals, posters, and statues throughout the country.**

most Western and moderate Arab countries supported Hussein at the beginning of his reign.

An Aggressive Warrior

Saddam Hussein rules Iraq with an iron fist and uses his secret police to crush internal opposition to his rule. Even close friends and relatives who are perceived to be a threat have been arrested, exiled, or killed.

Under Hussein's direction, Iraq attacked Iran in 1980, starting the Iran-Iraq War, in which Iraqi soldiers used chemical weapons against Iranian forces. In 1988, Hussein's forces again used chemical weapons, this time against their own people — the Kurds who had supported the Iranians in the war.

In 1998, the U.N. suspected Hussein of creating biological weapons and more chemical weapons. These rumors were substantiated when Hussein's son-in-law, Hussein Kamel, moved to Jordan and warned the world about these weapons. Although Hussein briefly cooperated with U.N. weapons inspectors, Kamel was murdered when he returned to Iraq. Many people believe that Saddam Hussein was behind the killing.

Above: **Although the Iraqi citizens suffer from a lack of basic necessities, Saddam Hussein continues to use the country's resources to build beautiful guest houses that are reserved for the exclusive use of his family and close supporters.**

The Iran-Iraq War

The Iran-Iraq War started on September 22, 1980, when Iraqi troops under the leadership of Saddam Hussein invaded neighboring Iran. The tension between the two countries had been building for many years and reflected a historic rivalry between Iraq and Iran for supremacy in the Persian Gulf area.

Hussein's main aim was for Iraq to take over control of the Shatt Al-Arab Waterway that separates the two countries. Another goal was for Iraq to claim Iran's Khuzestan province.

Just over two years into the war, in June 1982, the Iranian military proved to be too strong for the Iraqis, and Hussein withdrew his troops. This, however, did not mark the end of the conflict. In 1984, Iraq attacked ships sailing in the Persian Gulf, pulling other countries into the war. Iran responded by attacking ships that were transporting arms and weapons to Iraq.

Many countries were indirectly involved in the conflict. France and the former Soviet Union sold arms to Iraq, while Kuwait and other Gulf Arab states gave Hussein financial help. The U.S.

Below: **Iraqi soldiers prepare for battle during the eight-year-long Iran-Iraq War.**

Above: **During the Iran-Iraq War, the Iraqis used bulldozers to clear road barriers and dig through rubble.**

officially remained neutral, but helped both Iraq and Iran. Iraq was given military aid and intelligence information, while arms were secretly sold to Iran.

A Cease-fire

After the U.S. ship *Stark* was accidentally hit by an Iraqi missile in May 1987, the United States sent additional navy personnel to the Gulf and permitted eleven Kuwaiti tankers to fly the U.S. flag. Other countries also increased their military presence in the Gulf.

In July 1987, Iraq agreed to a U.N. resolution to stop the war. Iran also agreed to accept this resolution in July 1988. The Iraqi military, however, continued to launch both air and ground attacks on Iran. Both sides finally honored the cease-fire on August 20, 1988.

A Change of Mind

On August 15, 1990, two weeks after Iraq invaded Kuwait, Hussein informed the Iranian government that he agreed to all the points that Iran had fought for during the Iran-Iraq War. It is widely believed that Hussein conceded to Iran to prevent further threats from Iran as the U.S.-led coalition forces moved in to fight Iraqi forces during the Persian Gulf War.

Iraq's Oil Industry

Far beneath the surface of Iraq lie two of the country's most precious resources — oil and natural gas. Twenty years ago, Iraq was the world's second-largest producer of oil, second only to Saudi Arabia. Today, Iraq's oil output is minimal.

Iraq's most valuable industry remains the production of petroleum and natural gas, even though the country still cannot use it to its full advantage. Refineries are located in Baghdad, Basra, Al Hadithah, Khanaqin, Kirkuk, and Qayyarah.

Extensive bombing during the Iran-Iraq War and the Persian Gulf War has damaged both Iraq's oil fields and its oil companies' buildings. In addition, the economic sanctions imposed during and after the Gulf War have severely reduced the export of Iraqi oil.

Oil for Food

In 2001, Iraq signed an agreement with the U.N. to extend the oil-for-food program. This program was designed to help ease the suffering of Iraqi citizens affected by the economic sanctions. Under the program, the Iraqi government is allowed

Below: **Many of Iraq's pipelines that were damaged during the Persian Gulf War have since been repaired.**

to sell oil and use the money it earns to buy food, medicine, and other supplies that the Iraqi people desperately need.

To ensure that Iraq is using the profits correctly, the U.N. places the money earned from Iraqi oil sales in a special escrow bank account, which is closely monitored. Currently, Iraq sells two million barrels of crude oil per day through the U.N. system.

The Environment

Partly because the Iraqis do not have the proper equipment owing to the economic sanctions, their oil tankers tend to cause more oil spills than usual. Without enough money to properly feed its people, cleaning up the environment is low on Iraq's list of priorities.

In defiance of the sanctions, some Iraqi oil companies sell oil illegally. Some of these illegal deals have had a disastrous effect on the environment. In 2001, a ship smuggling 900 tons (817 metric tons) of Iraqi crude oil sank in the Persian Gulf, leaving behind a large oil slick. Although the spill did not reach the coast, it jeopardized marine life and polluted the waters of the Arabian Sea.

Above: **The smuggling of crude oil can have a disastrous effect on the environment. Sometimes the tankers sink or spring leaks that leave oil slicks such as this one that polluted the Arabian Sea and the surrounding coastal areas.**

The Kurds

The Kurds are an ethnic minority group that lives in northern Iraq. They can also be found in southeastern Turkey, northeastern Syria, and Azerbaijan. Kurds speak Kurdish and are mostly Sunni Muslims. The traditional Kurdish lifestyle was a nomadic one based on tending herds of sheep and goats, but most Kurds today work as farmers. Kurds are known for their colorful clothing, their lyrical poetry and music, and their intricate knitwear.

Broken Promises, Broken Dreams

After the Ottoman Empire collapsed in 1917, Turkey promised to create a separate homeland for the Kurds — to be called Kurdistan — when the Turkish government signed the Treaty of Sevres in 1920. Turkey, however, reneged on its promise, and Kurds have since been oppressed in every country in which they live.

Kurds dream of living in a country where they are free to speak their own language and nuture and promote their customs and traditions. The idea of Kurdistan, however, seems as much a dream today as when the proposal was first suggested in 1917.

Below: **Although Kurdistan as a nation is not officially recognized, the Kurds have erected "Welcome to Kurdistan" signs in northern Iraq, where the majority of them make their homes.**

Left: **As a result of persecution by the government and bombings that have destroyed their houses, many Iraqi Kurds have been forced to leave their homes and live in refugee camps located both in Iraq and in other countries, such as Turkey.**

The Kurds fought for their rights against Iraqi troops throughout the 1960s. In 1970, the Iraqi government agreed to let the Kurds govern themselves and allowed them to make Arbil their capital. The Kurds rejected this proposal because they did not believe that Iraq would honor the agreement.

In 1980, the Kurds received minimal representation in government when Saddam Hussein formed the 50-member Kurdish Legislative Council.

Persecuted

Throughout the 1980s, Saddam Hussein led military attacks against many Iraqi Kurds because he feared they would take part in an uprising against him. The worst massacre happened in 1988 when Iraq's military unleashed poisonous gas on several Kurdish villages, killing 5,000 Kurds. After this incident, some of the surviving Kurds fled across the border to Turkey.

The Iraqi Kurds rebelled again after the Persian Gulf War in 1991, but Iraqi troops quickly defeated the rebellion. Again, many Kurds fled Iraq. Aided by the countries that made up the coalition forces that fought Iraq in 1991, most Iraqi Kurds have since returned to their homes.

Mosul: City of Diversity

Mosul is Iraq's third largest city and the capital of Ninawa province. Due to its location along the Tigris River, the city started out as an important trading center during the reign of King Ashurnasirpal II in about 850 B.C. Caravans often stopped there on the way to India and the Mediterranean Sea.

Over the years, Mosul endured conquerors from many different lands, such as Mongols, Persians, and Turks. The city was part of the Ottoman Empire from 1534 to 1917, and afterward, the British controlled it until 1920. Mosul became part of Iraq in 1926.

A Diverse City

Located 220 miles (354 km) from Baghdad, Mosul is a city where peoples of different cultures have settled. Although most people

Below: **The city of Mosul is located in northern Iraq. Mosul is known as "the City of Two Springs" because its weather in fall is similar to its weather in spring.**

who live in Mosul are Arabs, many Kurds and Christians also reside in the city. Famous for its ancient neighborhoods, Mosul also features several modern buildings and is home to Mosul University, founded in 1967.

Above: **The Great Mosque in Mosul was built in the eleventh century and was once considered a major tourist attraction.**

Ruins

The city of Mosul boasts many archaeological ruins. In 1840, Sir Austen Henry Layard discovered stones inscribed with cuneiform letters, among other items. These stones turned out to be from the palace of King Sennacherib (r.705B.C.–681B.C.) and his grandson, Ashurbanipal (r.668B.C.–627B.C.). Other archaeological sites in the area include the ancient cities of Nineveh, located across the Tigris River, and Hatra, situated to the southwest of Mosul.

City of Mosques and Castles

Not all of Mosul's treasures lie underground. Iraqis flock to see its three great ancient mosques: the Great Mosque, the Red Mosque, and the Mosque of Nabi Jarjis. Mosul is also home to many historic castles, churches, and monasteries.

The Persian Gulf War

On August 2, 1990, Iraqi military forces invaded Kuwait, and Saddam Hussein then declared Kuwait as Iraq's nineteenth province. To justify the invasion, Hussein claimed that Kuwait actually belonged to Iraq. While it was true that Kuwait belonged to the Ottoman province of Basra until the collapse of the Ottoman Empire in 1918, the borders of Iraq were not formed until after World War I. In addition, Iraq's government had officially recognized Kuwait's independence in 1963. Hussein also alleged that Kuwait was illegally siphoning oil from Iraqi oil fields, but this was never proven.

The U.N. Security Council passed 12 resolutions that condemned Iraq's invasion and agreed that force could be used if Iraqi troops did not withdraw peacefully from Kuwait by January 15, 1991. Following Iraq's refusal to withdraw, the Persian Gulf War officially began on January 16, 1991.

The U.S.-led military coalition formed to drive Iraq from Kuwait consisted of different nations from all over the world. The United States contributed the largest force, sending 500,000

Below: **U.S. troops get ready to go to war with Iraq. Note the special camouflage uniforms designed to help the soldiers blend with the desert terrain.**

Left: The Persian Gulf War was unique as it was the first time that media coverage lasted 24 hours a day and enabled viewers all over the world to witness the bombings and the ground war live on television. These coalition soldiers in Kuwait clear buildings of enemy troops and search for enemy ammunition.

troops, 1,800 aircraft, and 100 ships into the area. The U.S. landed in Saudi Arabia to begin a mission called Operation Desert Shield to protect Saudi Arabia and its neighbors from Iraqi invasions. In November 1990, when the coalition's forces started to use force to drive the Iraqis from Kuwait, they renamed the mission Operation Desert Storm.

To minimize the number of causalities, American coalition commander General Norman Schwarzkopf conducted the attack mainly by air, dropping guided missiles on Iraqi military targets. Schwarzkopf, however, knew that they would eventually have to fight a more dangerous war on the ground.

The ground war, which started on February 23, lasted only 100 hours. Schwarzkopf deployed a huge number of forces to southwestern Iraq, from where the troops moved to surround Iraqi forces in Kuwait and southern Iraq. The Iraqi forces, who had been greatly weakened after five weeks of air raids, were quickly overpowered. At midnight on February 28, following the Iraqi troops retreat from Kuwait, U.S. president George H.W. Bush declared the end of the ground war.

Though the Persian Gulf War only lasted a short time, it has had a big impact on Iraq. After the war, the country's economy collapsed as a result of the U.N.-imposed economic sanctions that brought a stop to Iraq's trade with other nations.

Sumerian Inventions

An ancient people who moved to the area between the Tigris and Euphrates rivers about 3500 B.C., the Sumerians — and their inventions — have had a great impact on subsequent societies and cultures. The basis of much of modern technology can be traced back to the inventions of the Sumerians.

The Write Stuff

Perhaps the Sumerians' greatest invention was the art of writing. Their early wedge-shaped characters, called cuneiform, were made by pressing a stylus into a clay tablet, which was then baked in the sun to dry. At first, these characters were visual symbols, similar to those used in Asian languages. Over time, the writing style changed and the characters eventually represented syllables.

Transportation and Tools

One creation of the Sumerians was the sailboat. Although the early sailboats were probably simple vessels, the invention made it possible for the Sumerians to trade with faraway countries.

The Sumerians also created the invention that is the basis of modern transportation and machinery — the wheel. Initially

Below: **Archaeologists have discovered artifacts and building walls from ancient times that are covered with cuneiform writing. Cuneiform takes its name from the Latin word** *cuneus,* **meaning "wedge," as its letters have wedged shapes.**

simple carts were designed to move heavy loads easily. Later inventions such as the chariot were more complex.

Sumerian farmers invented the plow, which also used the wheel. Early plows were first crafted from stone and later from copper. The Sumerians also created hoes and spades, the same tools that gardeners use today.

Above: **The Sumerians were very advanced in building techniques and succeeded in building massive temples, such as this one at Ur. Each temple, called a ziggurat, was dedicated to a specific god.**

Right on Time

The idea of time keeping was another Sumerian creation. The Sumerians invented a calendar that divided the year into 30-day months, divided the day into twelve periods, and divided each of these twelve periods into thirty parts.

Law and Order

Another essential Sumerian invention was the idea of law. They realized that their society needed a series of written rules to make sure their citizens behaved correctly.

Many Sumerians inventions are still in use today, proving that the Sumerians' ideas have indeed stood the test of time.

A Tale of Two Rivers

Iraq, a country of deserts, also has two major rivers — the Tigris and the Euphrates — running through its land. Not only do these rivers supply Iraqis with water for drinking, agriculture, and transportation, they also boast rich and varied histories.

Flowing for 1,180 miles (1,900 km), the Tigris runs through Iraq and Turkey. With its source at Turkey's Lake Golcuk, the Tigris flows southeast into the Iraqi city of Mosul before tracing its path to Baghdad and Al-Qurnah. The Tigris meets the Euphrates at Al-Qurnah to form the Shatt Al-Arab Waterway, which drains into the Persian Gulf. The Tigris is accessible to boats between Baghdad and Al-Qurnah.

The Euphrates's source lies at the intersection of two smaller rivers, the Kara Su and the Murat, in Turkey. The river then flows through Syria and enters central Iraq. In Iraq, the Euphrates's path narrows as it flows through breathtaking limestone cliffs

Below: **The Euphrates River starts as a strong steady stream of water, but as it flows across Iraq, the river becomes gentler. It begins to wind near the ancient city of Babylon.**

Above: **The land along the lower reaches of the Tigris River has rich alluvial soil that is suitable for farming.**

until it reaches Hit. At this point, the Euphrates flows through an alluvial flood plain consisting of layers that are the result of sediment left behind by floods in the area over the years.

The Fertile Crescent: A Disappearing Act

Part of the area at the intersection of Iraq's two mighty rivers is known as the Fertile Crescent. This crescent-shaped band of land has been home to some of the world's earliest advanced civilizations. As its name suggests, it was a fertile piece of land where farmers' crops grew abundantly.

Today, environmentalists fear that the Fertile Crescent will disappear because excessive damming and draining have caused the original land to dry up. Only a small piece of the original Fertile Crescent, located along the Iraq-Iran border remains.

The Flooding Season

The Euphrates floods just after the rainy season that usually occurs between April and May. When the Euphrates floods, small "temporary lakes" crop up all along the flood plain. They eventually dry up when the hot summer season arrives.

RELATIONS WITH NORTH AMERICA

Iraq and North America do not enjoy good relations. While many North Americans feel bad about the hardships that the U.N. sanctions have brought to the Iraqi people, they generally regard Saddam Hussein as a ruthless dictator who is largely to blame for his people's suffering. Iraq views the United States, and the West in general, as standing against the Muslim world — particularly with respect to Iraq — in terms of economics, culture, and politics.

Despite their poor political relations, North Americans and Iraqis have some things in common, such as an appreciation for art and culture. American museums such as New York's Metropolitan Museum of Art and Philadelphia's University of Pennsylvania Museum of Archaeology and Anthropology feature displays of exquisite treasures from Iraq's past that are well received by Americans. Many Iraqi emigrants also choose to start new lives in Canada and the United States.

Opposite: **As the media in Iraq is controlled by the government, most Iraqi people continue to believe that the United States is responsible for the country's problems. These schoolgirls hold placards to protest against the United States outside their school in Baghdad.**

Below: **In 1994, the United States sent the USS *George Washington*, an aircraft carrier, to the Persian Gulf in order to enforce the U.N.-imposed sanctions against Iraq.**

A Tense Relationship

Relations between the United States and Iraq, while mostly tense, have not always been as eruptive as they have been since the end of the Persian Gulf War in April 1991. In fact, the two countries even shared an alliance for a brief moment in history.

From 1973 to 1975, the United States secretly gave military support to the Iraqi Kurds in their internal revolts against the Iraqi government. The United States, however, refused scores of Kurdish refugees in 1975, when Iran was forced to close its border because it was unable to cope with the sheer number of refugees.

When Iraq invaded Iran in 1980, the United States did not take any action against Iraq, as the United States and Iran were on even less friendly terms. The Iraqi invasion developed into the Iran-Iraq War (1980–1988). During that time, the United States took Iraq off its list of nations that supported terrorism and even provided the country with some weapons. In 1987, U.S. naval forces sailed into the Persian Gulf on the side of Iraq.

Below: **This picture taken in 1985 shows two Iraqi soldiers keeping watch during the Iran-Iraq War. Although the United States remained neutral in this conflict, the country supplied Iraq with intelligence information and military aid.**

Relations Deteriorate

The United States spearheaded the international coalition that took part in the Persian Gulf War against Iraq. In 1990, the U.N. imposed economic sanctions on Iraq to force them to withdraw their forces from Kuwait. After the end of the war in 1991, the economic sanctions were extended to prevent Iraq from both rearming its military and creating weapons of mass destruction.

The Persian Gulf War and the continued sanctions marked the official end of Iraq's diplomatic relations with the United States. Since then, the two countries have been at bitter odds. Iraq has long blamed the West — and the United States, in particular — for its sorry economic state. In return, the United States has accused Iraq of state-sponsored terrorism.

The No-fly Zones

In 1991, the United States created a "no-fly zone" over southern Iraq after the Persian Gulf War to diminish Iraq's ability to threaten Kuwait or Saudi Arabia, and to protect Shi'ite Muslims living in the south from attack by Saddam Hussein's military. Another no-fly zone was established over northern Iraq in 1992 to protect Iraqi Kurds in that area from government air attacks.

Above: **An American soldier in Iraq talks on a field telephone during the Persian Gulf War.**

Helping Iraq's People

In 1996, the U.N. acknowledged the devastating effect the economic sanctions were having on the Iraqi people. It decided to permit Iraq to sell oil in return for medicine, food, and other necessary supplies. Saddam Hussein initially rejected this plan but later accepted it.

In 1997, the U.N. Security Council sent arms inspectors to Iraq when it learned that the country was allegedly still creating chemical and biological weapons. Hussein and his government proved to be extremely uncooperative and would not allow the inspection of many sites on the inspectors' list. This led the U.S. and its allies to believe that Iraq had something to hide, and they announced that possible military action was being considered against Iraq.

In February 1998, the government of Canada announced its contribution of the patrol frigate HMCS *Toronto* and two KC10 tactical air-to-air refueling planes to possible military action in

Below: Under the U.N. Oil-for-Food program, Iraq is allowed to use the money gained from selling oil to buy food. Although this Iraqi man carries sacks of food in a Baghdad market, there is still a severe food shortage in Iraq because the government has chosen to import less than what is needed.

Left: In view of the uncertain conditions in Iraq, many of its citizens who are professionals, such as these two women, have chosen to emigrate to the United States and Canada and start a new life.

the Persian Gulf. Canadian prime minister Jean Chrétien said sending military aircraft to the Persian Gulf reflected Canada's commitment to seek a means to bring Iraq into compliance with U.N. Security Council resolutions.

The U.N. weapons inspectors eventually pulled out of Iraq in December 1998, their mission incomplete.

Iraqi Emigration to North America

As of the U.S. population census conducted in 1990, 20,657 persons of Iraqi ancestry lived in the United States. Of these, 6,298 were born in the United States. Most Iraqi immigrants are well-educated and work in the professional and business worlds.

Since the Persian Gulf War of 1991, thousands of Iraqi immigrants have sought refuge in North America. Currently, Iraqi immigrants make up the fifth-largest Arab group in the United States. About 60 percent of these people are Assyrians, most of whom are Christians. Recently, many Iraqis have attempted to gain asylum in the United States at the Mexican border.

"Little Iraq" in the United States

Many Iraqis have settled in Arab communities in Nebraska and Washington, D.C., as well as in larger cities such as New York and Los Angeles. Since the Persian Gulf War, Detroit has served as the point of entry into the United States for over three thousand Iraqis each year. The area around Dearborn, Michigan, has the largest Arab community in the United States and is home to about 400,000 Arab-Americans.

Many shops in Dearborn are Arab-American-owned and feature signs and information in both Arabic and English. Residents can also worship at local mosques and take part in many Arab-American cultural activities. In fact, many teachers even give lessons to children in both Arabic and English.

Culture Clash

Iraqis' adjustment to the American way of life is not always smooth. Besides the difficulties involved with learning a new language, adjusting to a new culture, and being far away from friends and family, some Iraqi immigrants have met hostility in their new homeland.

Below: **Younger Iraqis have an easier time adapting to cultural differences when they immigrate to North America than the older generations of Iraqis.**

Above: **In 2001, the Catholic group Voices in the Wilderness made one of its many visits to Iraq. Kathy Kelly, a spokesperson for the group, gives a toy to an Iraqi boy at Baghdad's al-Mansur Children's Hospital.**

Bridging the Cultural Gap

The American-based Iraqi Foundation launched the Iraqi Community Organization Project (ICOP) to help refugees adjust to their new environment, acquire necessary skills, and integrate into American society. At the same time, it allows them to hold onto their culture and traditions and create a sense of community.

North Americans in Iraq

In view of the recent hostilities between Iraq and North America, few Westerners venture into Iraq. In fact, Americans are forbidden by the U.S. Department of State to visit Iraq. Recently, however, some groups who oppose the economic sanctions have defied this law and entered Iraq, bearing gifts of food and hopes for peace.

A delegation of American Catholics called Voices in the Wilderness has made numerous delegations to Iraq. In 1999, they even spent Christmas in a Basra Christian community, where they visited hospitals and sick Iraqi children.

A Canadian group called Voices of Conscience visited Iraq in 2000. The Iraqis were given gifts of medical supplies such as sterilized gloves, aspirin, and local anesthetics.

Current Relations

Relations between the United States and Iraq are as bad as ever. The United States has suggested that Iraq was involved in the terrorist attacks on it on September 11, 2001. Although evidence shows that Iraq is one of the nations that sponsors terrorism, no direct ties between the September 11 attacks and the country have yet been disclosed. Records, however, show that Mohammed Atta, one of the terrorist pilots who steered an airplane into one of the World Trade Center towers, met at least twice with an Iraqi intelligence officer in Prague in the Czech Republic.

Below: In 2002, citizens of the city of Baghdad held a demonstration to mark the anniversary of U.S. intervention in the Persian Gulf region. The people hold up the Iraqi flag and portraits of their president, Saddam Hussein, as they burn the American flag.

Above: A U.N. weapons inspection team is greeted with signs reading "Down USA" as it arrives at an airport on the outskirts of Baghdad in 1997.

More Inspections

The U.N. is planning to once again send weapons inspectors into Iraq. Their action is in response to the statement by an Iraqi defector named Adnan Ihsan Saeed al-Haideri, who admitted to working at a biological, nuclear, and chemical weapons plant in Iraq.

Iraq's Arab neighbors in the Persian Gulf region, including Bahrain, Kuwait, Oman, Qatar, Saudi Arabia, and the United Arab Emirates, are urging Hussein to comply with the U.N. weapons inspections for fear of another war in the region.

Relations Continue to Deteriorate

On January 15, 2002, U.S. senator Joseph Lieberman hinted that action against Iraq might be necessary, with the aim of ousting Saddam Hussein.

During his State of the Union Address to the American people on January 29, 2002, President George W. Bush also had strong words against Iraq.

Above: U.S. president George W. Bush spoke out against Iraq during his State of the Union address in 2002.

Art: The Universal Language

Even though Iraq and North America might disagree on politics, people from all of these places can appreciate the universal, peaceful language of the arts. Recently, at the Henry Ford Centennial Library in Dearborn, Michigan, many Arab-American artists, including Iraqi artist Mohammed Fradi, displayed and sold their work. Visitors enjoyed the artworks, and the artists enjoyed the opportunity to exhibit without government censorship.

Americans also got a glimpse of the work of another contemporary Iraqi artist in 1999. Dr. Khalid Al-Qassab exhibited his watercolor paintings at the Arab Cultural Center in San Francisco, California.

Below: **College students of Iraqi origin in the United States pose for a photograph at an exhibition organized to raise awareness of Iraqi art and culture in their newly adopted home.**

A Gathering of Cultures

Cultural fairs such as the Dearborn Arab International Festival serve two purposes. Besides helping Iraqi-Americans stay in touch with their cultural roots, they also give Americans a rare glimpse at Iraqi culture and a chance to make friends with Iraqis and find some common ground. At the fairs, Americans get a chance to speak to Iraqis, taste traditional Iraqi foods, hear Iraqi music, and view Iraqi children performing traditional dances.

Above: **Iraqis who have settled in the United States organize regular cultural programs, such as musical recitals. These programs enable younger Iraqis to stay in touch with their roots and provide American citizens with an opportunity to learn about Iraqi culture.**

A Good Sport

While Canada and Iraq do not have any official diplomatic relations, the two nations have met in the sporting arena. In June 2001, during the World Under-20 Soccer Championship, Canada and Iraq played against each other. The match was won by the Iraqi team, which beat the Canadian team 3-0.

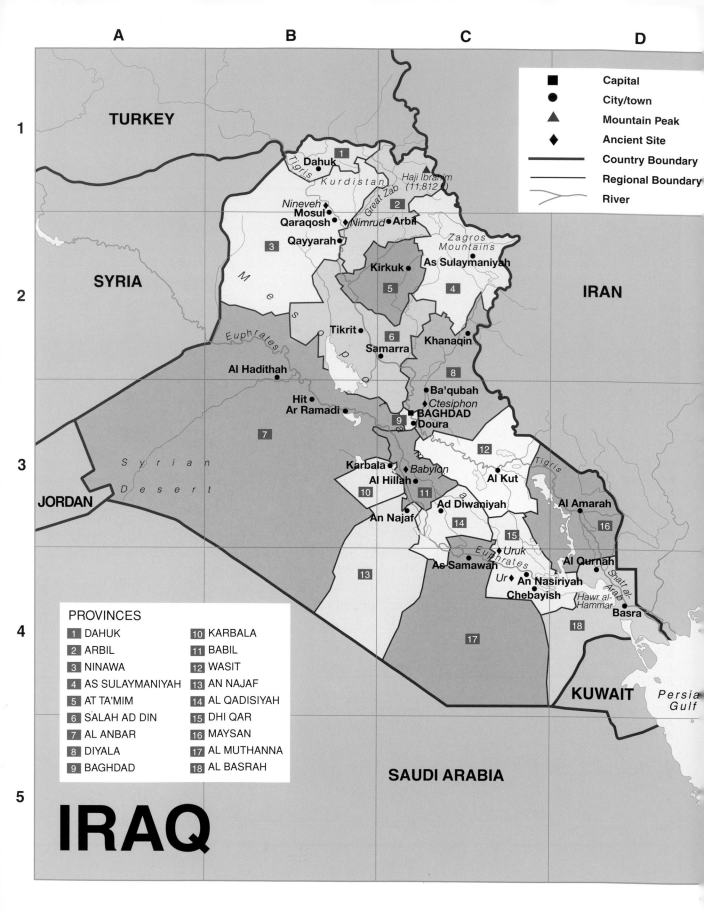

TURKEY

1

Dahuk ●

Kurdistan

Haji Ibrahim
(11,812 ft)

Tigris

Great Zab

1

SYRIA

Nineveh ♦
Mosul ●
Arbil ●
Qaraqosh ●
♦ *Nimrud*

2

Qayyarah ●

3

M
e
s
o

2

Kirkuk ●

5

As Sulaymaniyah ●

4

Zagros
Mountains

IRAN

2

Euphrates

Tikrit ●

6

Samarra ●

Khanaqin ●

8

Al Hadithah ●

Hit ●
Ar Ramadi ●

7

Ba'qubah ●
♦ *Ctesiphon*
9 ■**BAGHDAD**
●**Doura**

12

Tigris

3

Syrian

Desert

JORDAN

Karbala ●
Al Hillah ●
♦ *Babylon*

10

11

Al Kut ●

Al Amarah ●

16

An Najaf ●

14

Ad Diwaniyah ●

15

Euphrates
♦ *Uruk*

Al Qurnah ●

3

13

As Samawah ●

Ur ♦
An Nasiriyah ●
Chebayish ●

Hawr al-
Hammar

Shatt al-
Arab

Basra ●

17

18

4

KUWAIT

Persia
Gulf

SAUDI ARABIA

5

IRAQ

Legend:
■ Capital
● City/town
▲ Mountain Peak
♦ Ancient Site
— Country Boundary
— Regional Boundary
〰 River

Above: A typical Marsh Arab home is constructed using natural materials, such as reed, that are commonly found beside rivers.

Ad Diwaniyah C3
Al Amarah D3
Al Anbar (province) A3–C3
Al Basrah (province) C4–D4
Al Hadithah B2
Al Hillah C3
Al Kut C3
Al Muthanna (province) C4
Al Qadisiyah (province) C3
Al Qurnah D4
An Najaf (city) C3
An Najaf (province) B4–C3
An Nasiriyah C4
Ar Ramadi B3
Arbil (city) C2
Arbil (province) B2–C1
As Samawah C4
As Sulaymaniyah (city) C2
As Sulaymaniyah (province) C2
At Ta'mim (province) B2–C2

Babil (province) C3
Babylon C3

Baghdad (city) C3
Baghdad (province) C3
Ba'qubah C3
Basra D4

Chebayish C4
Ctesiphon C3

Dahuk (city) B1
Dahuk (province) B1
Dhi Qar (province) C3–D4
Diyala (province) C2–C3
Doura C3

Euphrates River B2–C4

Great Zab River B2–C1

Haji Ibrahim C1
Hawr al Hammar C4–D4
Hit B3

Iran C1–D4

Jordan A3

Karbala (city) C3
Karbala (province) B3-C3
Khanaqin C2
Kirkuk C2

Kurdistan B1
Kuwait D4

Maysan (province) C4-D3
Mesopotamia B2–C3
Mosul B1

Nimrud B2
Ninawa (province) B1–B2
Nineveh B1

Persian Gulf D4–D5

Qaraqosh B2
Qayyarah B2

Salah ad Din (province) B2–C3
Samarra C2
Saudi Arabia A3–D5
Shatt Al-Arab Waterway D4
Syria A1–B2

Tigris River B1–D4
Tikrit B2
Turkey A1–C1

Ur C4
Uruk C4

Wasit (province) C3

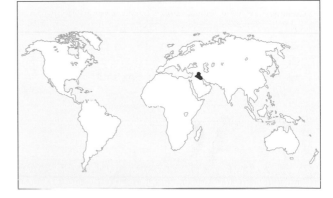

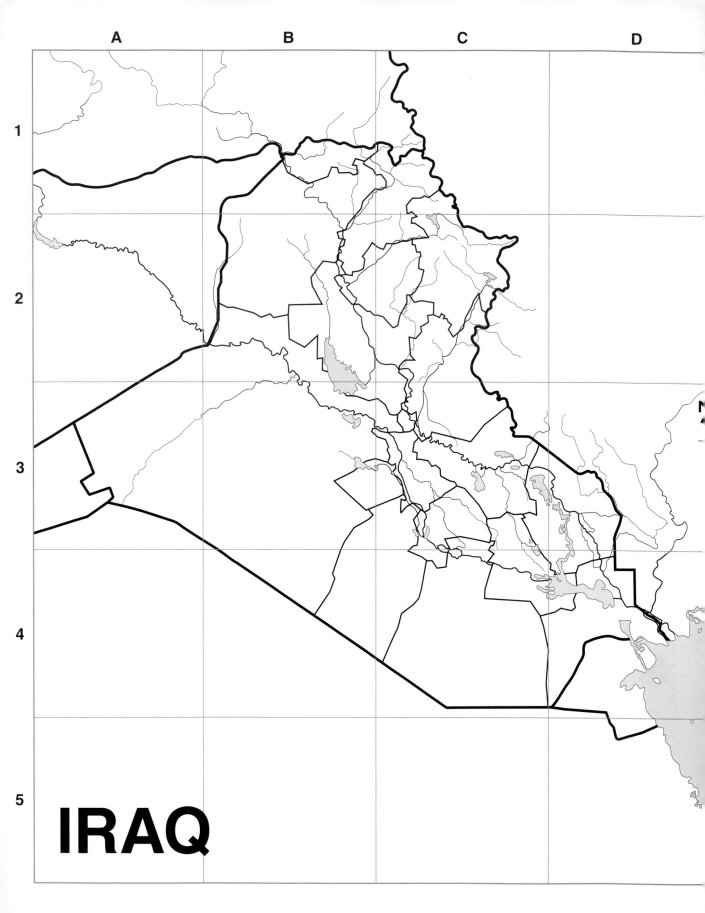

A B C D

1

2

3

4

5

IRAQ

How Is Your Geography?

Learning to identify the main geographical areas and points of a country can be challenging. Although it may seem difficult at first to memorize the locations and spellings of major cities or the names of mountain ranges, rivers, deserts, lakes, and other prominent physical features, the end result of this effort can be very rewarding. Places you previously did not know existed will suddenly come to life when referred to in world news, whether in newspapers, television reports, other books and reference sources, or on the Internet. This knowledge will make you feel a bit closer to the rest of the world, with its fascinating variety of cultures and physical geography.

Used in a classroom setting, the instructor can make duplicates of this map using a copy machine. (PLEASE DO NOT WRITE IN THIS BOOK!) Students can then fill in any requested information on their individual map copies. Used one-on-one, the student can also make copies of the map on a copy machine and use them as a study tool. The student can practice identifying place names and geographical features on his or her own.

Above: The Monument to the Dead in the city of Baghdad is dedicated to Iraqi soldiers who lost their lives in the Iran-Iraq War.

Iraq at a Glance

Official Name   Republic of Iraq

Capital   Baghdad

Official Language   Arabic

Population   23,331,985 (July 2001)

Area   168,710 square miles (437,072 sq km)

Provinces   Al Anbar, Al Basrah, Al Muthanna, Al Qadisiyah, An Najaf, Arbil, As Sulaymaniyah, At Ta'mim, Babil, Baghdad, Dahuk, Dhi Qar, Diyala, Karbala, Maysan, Ninawa, Salah ad Din, Wasit

Bordering Countries   Iran, Jordan, Kuwait, Saudi Arabia, Syria, Turkey

Highest Point   Haji Ibrahim 11,812 feet (3,600 m)

Major Cities   Baghdad, Basra, Mosul

Major Rivers   Euphrates, Tigris

Major Lake   Hawr al-Hammar

Official Religion   Islam

Public Holidays   New Year's Day (January 1), Army Day (January 6), Revolution Anniversary (February 8), FAO Day (April 17), Labour Day (May 1), National Day (July 14), Ba'ath Revolution Day (July 17), Peace Day (August 8)

Religious Holidays   Ashura, Eid al-Adha, Eid al-Fitr, Islamic New Year, Prophet Muhammad's birthday

Famous Leaders   King Faisal I (1885–1933), King Faisal II (1935–1958), Nuri es-Said (1888–1958), Saddam Hussein (1937–)

National Anthem   Land of Two Rivers

Natural Resources   Natural gas, petroleum, phosphates, sulfur

Currency   Iraqi dinar (0.31 dinar = U.S.$1)

Opposite: **Due to their physical characteristics, camels are able to survive in harsh desert conditions.**

Glossary

Arabic Vocabulary

abbayah (ah-BYE-ah): a long black gown and veil worn by Muslim women that completely covers their bodies and hair.

Allahu akbar (ah-LAH-who-AHK-bar): God is great.

Ashura (ah-SHOO-rah): A Shi'ite holiday in rememberence of a religious martyr named Imam Hussein who was put to death for his beliefs.

baklava (baa-KLAH-vah): a rich pastry made of layers of honey, thin sheets of buttery dough, and nuts.

Eid al-Adha (EAD al-AD-hah): feast of the sacrifice, a major Muslim holiday.

Eid al-Fitr (EAD al-FIT-er): feast of the breaking of the fast that takes place at the end of the month of Ramadan.

khanjars (CAN-jars): daggers carried by Kurdish men.

kibba (kih-BAH): deep-fried balls of ground meat, nuts, raisins, and spices.

Ma'dan (MAH-dan): the Arabs who live in the marshy area of Iraq.

masgouf (MAS-goof): an Iraqi fish dish in which the fish is skewered and cooked slowly over a fire made from sweet woods.

mudhif (mood-HEEF): a guest house in the Ma'dan community.

mukhabarat (mook-hob-BAH-rot): the secret police in Iraq.

murabba amar (moor-ah-bah AH-mar): a dessert in which dates are soaked in syrup.

mushtamal (moosh-TAH-mal): an extension that is built onto an Iraqi home to house more family members.

oud (OUD): a stringed musical instrument that is shaped like a gourd.

quzi (KOO-zee): a dish of stuffed roasted lamb.

rebaba (rah-BAH-bah): a single-stringed musical instrument shaped like a fiddle that is usually played by the Bedouin.

rigg (RIG-g): an Iraqi-style tambourine.

salah (SALL-ah): the requirement to pray five times a day in the direction of Mecca; one of the five pillars of Islam.

samoons (SAH-moons): traditional flat bread, usually dusted with either poppy or sesame seeds, that accompanies most Iraqi meals.

sawm (SAH-m): the act of fasting; one of the five pillars of Islam.

shahada (SHA-hah-dah): the declaration of a Muslim's faith that states "There is no god but Allah, and Muhammad the prophet is His messenger"; one of the five pillars of Islam.

shamal (sham-ALL): a type of wind that usually blows in Iraq between June and September.

sharqi (shar-KEE): the wind that blows across southern Iraq, reaching speeds of up to 50 miles (80 km) per hour.

Yazidis (yahd-ZEE-deez): a minority Arabic group that lives in northwestern Iraq.

zakat (zah-COT): the giving of alms to the poor; one of the five pillars of Islam.

zlabiya (zlah-BEE-yah): date pastries.

English Vocabulary

abstinence: the refraining from certain types of food.

alluvial: made of material deposited by running water.

arabesque: an ornamental style in which flowers and other designs are represented in intricate patterns.

autonomous: self-governing.

biological weapons: devices that spread highly contagious germs in order to harm people.

black market: an illegal or unofficial system of trade that operates without a government's knowledge.

bulgur: parched cracked wheat.

calligraphy: the art of using special pens to produce beautiful handwriting.

commissions: orders given to artists or craftspeople by clients to produce particular works.

coup d'état: an unexpected political uprising, usually using force.

cuneiform: an ancient system of writing that uses wedge-shaped letters, formed by pressing a stylus into a clay tablet.

curtailed: limited or cut short.

dictator: a ruler of a country or state who excercises absolute power without the consent of the people.

economic sanctions: measures taken by a country or organization to restrict trade with a nation that has broken international law.

embroidery: the art of ornamenting cloth or other material using a needle and thread.

embroiled: involved in conflict.

escrow: money that is held in a special account for safekeeping.

free verse: a form of poetry in which the lines do not rhyme.

gourd: the hard-shelled fruit of any plant belonging to the gourd family.

hajj: a pilgrimage to the holy city of Mecca, Saudi Arabia, that every Muslim is expected to make at least once in his or her life.

humidity: the percentage of water vapor in the air.

kabobs: skewered chunks of grilled lamb, beef, chicken, or fish.

mandate: authority over a country.

no-fly zones: areas that aircraft are prohibited from flying over, usually to protect the people living below from being attacked by air.

nomads: people with no fixed homes who wander from place to place.

plebiscite: a vote in which citizens decide for or against a proposal.

refineries: buildings with equipment for purifying crude oil.

reneged: went back on.

stele: an upright stone slab or pillar bearing an inscription or design that also serves as a monument or marker.

taboo: something that is deemed improper or unacceptable by society.

trills: rolling sounds made with the tongue.

unicameral: consisting of one legislative chamber or house.

wadis: channels of a river that are dry except during periods of heavy rainfall.

More Books to Read

Daily Life in Ancient and Modern Baghdad. Cities Through Time series.
   Dawn Kotapish (Lerner)

Iraq. Countries Faces and Places series. Kathryn Stevens (Child's World)

Iraq. Major World Nations series. J.P. Docherty (Chelsea House)

Iraq: Old Land, New Nation in Conflict. William Spencer
   (Twenty First Century Books)

Mesopotamia. Ancient Civilizations series. Tami Deedrick
   (Raintree/Steck-Vaughn)

Looking Back: Mesopotamia and the Fertile Crescent. Mavis Pilbeam
   (Raintree/Steck-Vaughn)

The Revenge of Ishtar. Ludmila Zeman (Tundra Books)

Science in Ancient Mesopotamia. Carol Moss (Franklin Watts)

The War against Iraq. American War Library series. Don Nardo
   (Lucent Books)

Videos

Ancient Mesopotamia. Ancient Civilizations for Children series. (Schlessinger)

Iran and Iraq. 20th Century with Mike Wallace series. (The History Channel)

Saddam Hussein vs. the Coalition. (ABC News)

Web Sites

www.arab.net/iraq/iraq_contents.html

www.arab.de/arab/Arab_Countries/Iraq/

www.mit.edu:80001/activities/arab/multimedia/iraq-pictures.html

Due to the dynamic nature of the Internet, some web sites stay current longer than others. To find additional web sites, use a reliable search engine with one or more of the following keywords to help you locate information about Iraq. Keywords: *Baghdad, Basra, economic sanctions, Mesopotamia, oil, Persian Gulf War, Saddam Hussein.*

Index